F the Norm

MICHAEL FABBER

Copyright © 2019 by Michael Fabber

All rights reserved.

ISBN 978-162806-285-4 (print | paperback)

Library of Congress Control Number 2020910214

Published by Salt Water Media
29 Broad Street, Suite 104
Berlin, MD 21811
www.saltwatermedia.com

Cover design by Evan Anderson
Images used are within the public domain and/or used with proper citiation; images for Chapters 1, 3, and 8 are courtesy of unsplash.com users Manasvita S., Milada Vigerova, and Wilhelm Gunkel.

Dedication

Literally for me to be at this place in my life this very moment there are countless people I should be dedicating this book to. I am grateful for all that inspire, challenge, motivate and push me to be greater because there would be no me without you.

The first book was dedicated to my mom and dad for being the beginning. They truly are the best anyone could ask for. That doesn't mean we didn't have a run in from time to time, but that is life.

This book is dedicated to the woman that saved my life 16 years ago. My daughter, Briana. You saved my life and became my life in a heart beat. You make me want to be better daily and grow into the dad you deserve, and that I fear I will never be. You inspire me. The world is brighter with you and I haven't met many with the pure heart you have. I am not sure why the big guns upstairs sends his best for me but he does time after time and you are no exception. I would not be near what I am today if I was not blessed with you. Always remember you are kind, strong, smart and capable of anything you

set your heart and mind to. I cannot wait to see how you change this world for the better. When you came to this world I knew you were the best part of my masterpiece and you prove me right daily. Thank you and I love you ... Always.

Also I got to give a shout out to my team and the UnleashU family. They make this all possible and so much more. They are the best of the best without any question. Ask how do you have over half a dozen businesses and keep up with all the projects and my answer is easy, them. They are truly amazing. I am lucky to have them. They are the heartbeat of change and the path to the life of your dreams. I am not worthy to have such amazing people with me on this journey but I am damn sure grateful I do. So I can't say from my heart bc you guys are part of my heart. So thank you for being the best and letting me be part of it. You guys rock!

As always this is dedicated to all those that didn't make it this far in the journey. For all those we carry with us still to this day. The ones we love without seeing because we still feel them. I hope we make you proud daily every day. Miss and love you guys...

My pops, Joey, Mat Carter, Ferris, Wig, Matt Allen and many more, here is to you.

My Brother, Joey

Above: My Parents
Below, Left to Right: Anthony Ferris, Mat Carter, Chris Wiggins

Foreword

Michael has the natural ability to uplift, inspire, and steer others into the direction of their most meaningful life, and he does this by simplifying key things that one needs to change in order to get there. He is not just forming kind words on a page; he is sincerely cheering us on to become better people; his message will remain long after you finish reading his book and so will his determination to connect his passion to our individual journey. He plants a constant reminder to be truer to ourselves no matter the opinions or actions of others.

It is an honest approach to life's winding road of failures, tragedy, and obstacles. Most importantly, it is a story about being willing to learn from your relationship to all things, such as the people you keep around you. We can only grow by learning. He shares his own personal stories with touches of humor and how he discovered his calling.

He not only stresses the importance of finding your own purpose for yourself, but also how it is meant to touch others. He reaches his audience by his unwavering belief that he was born to help every person that he can. He has a contagious way of thinking that leads the way for any reader to find the courage to embrace their own gifts and to begin to live a better life, so we can build a better world.

He shows us that all great accomplishments come with setbacks and regret, but the only true hurdle we have is our own negative mindset: at times we are our own worst enemy, and the only thing blinding us from seeing our mountaintop is ourselves. His message is for those in need of a little encouragement to be honest with themselves no matter the excuses for why we cannot be. Our real journey begins when we accept our past and focus on where we are going instead of where we are right now. You not only owe it to yourself to be great but also to the next generations to come. Only you know what your best life looks like, so only you can create it. You can paint your best life with whatever colors you chose, only if they are your true colors.

Vincenza L. Fabber, PhD

Table of Contents

CHAPTER 1:
Day One 12

CHAPTER 2:
Thick Skin 18

CHAPTER 3:
Mirror, Mirror 32

CHAPTER 4:
#Squad Goals 46

CHAPTER 5:
It's Your Calling ... Answer It 60

CHAPTER 6:
Easy now, Tiger! My Grandmother Said, "Panzenza." .. 72

CHAPTER 7:
Embrace the Suck 84

CHAPTER 8:
You Are Your Job 100

CHAPTER 9:
Grow Through It 114

CHAPTER 10:
See It Till It's Real 128

CHAPTER 11:
Serenity 140

CHAPTER 12:
Timmy Said It: "Be Humble and Kind." 154

CHAPTER 13:
Your Masterpiece 168

CHAPTER 14:
The Dance 182

Chapter 1

DAY ONE

"You only live once, but if you do it right, once is enough." — Mae West

Today is day one. Now, I know you've probably heard that before, and No, it's not like every other cliche-line because this time it's true. If you've already started the journey of self-discovery or if you haven't, if you've already decided your purpose, your calling, your passion, your mountaintop, or your ultimate goal or if you haven't, if you jumped out of bed today with excitement or if you hit the snooze button a couple times ...

I hope you get the point, but if you haven't, wherever you are in your journey, today is day one. This is day one of the rest of your life, but it is also day one for when you change your thinking and the limitations you put on yourself. Today, we see how amazing you are and that you are capable of any life you want. The best part is it's all up to you.

As Pete Carroll, the coach for the Seattle Seahawks said, "You are the master of you." As I tried to express in my first book, *Your Story: You Have Every Reason to Quit but Don't* ... I know, it's my shameless plug, but I had to. In that book we all have a story. They are all alike and different in many ways. We all have things to share, and we all know we're not alone.

This book is different. In this book ... It isn't your story I want. It is your greatness. That is right. If you are reading this right now, you have greatness within you if you believe it or not. I'm not saying you have shown the world it yet, but you have it, and I want it out of you. There is no point in playing small anymore, and it's time to shed those limiting beliefs, doubts, and restrictions and anything else you put on yourself that holds you back. Heck, we were all born with the right, the ability, and the responsibility to be great and to change the world for the better.

No, I'm not blowing smoke. This isn't some rainbows and lollipops type of book. This is a real book, not one that will spit opinions for hundreds of pages. This is a fact book that will bring up people that did amazing things in many areas of life. Some you might have heard of, and some you may have not. But they are impacting the world in their unique way.

What is greatness if not leaving this place better than we found it? No man is born to be ordinary. That is a choice one makes for themselves. Today, we will no longer make the choice. If we play small like I stated earlier, we do not move the flag further for the next, and it is our job to move it further for the next generation, for our kids, for our grandkids, and for everybody.

Elon Musk is on record saying he believed both his space company and car company would fail, but that they would make it closer for someone else to be able to accomplish it. That is the kind of thinking that changes the world. The risk for the greater good is how we greater the good.

No, you aren't Elon Musk, and believe me, I'm actually happy you aren't. We already have one of him. We all need you to be yourself, but we need you to be the best you living your best life. How does you living your best life look to you? It makes you smile, right? It makes you wonder.

I'm not here to tell you that you'll need to spend every waking hour trying to create a new car, plane, computer, phone, space shuttle, or anything else. That's not the only way to be great. We have all heard of some amazing people that never invented anything, and believe me, I bet we all forgot some people that did invent things.

It is not about what you create that leaves an impact: it is about what you give. Oh, you don't believe me? Not sure about that last part being true? Okay. How many nuns do you know the name of off the top of your head? I'll give you a second. Many will only be able to name one: Mother Teresa. Why is that? Easy. She was the one that gave the most. She took the normal standard for nuns and pushed it beyond sight. She went above and beyond to give all she could and as much as she could. Believe me, if you know other ones, it's because they gave something to you that you'll hang onto for as long as possible, but it's all about what you give.

Listen, I could give you example after example, and I will. The only thing you need to know is you are capable of greatness. You were meant for it. Your best life is an amazing life. No matter where you are at this moment, it is not important. What will get you there is what you do now, now that you know there are no more excuses. You refuse to hold yourself back. Nothing is standing between you and your wildest dreams as long as you don't. The only thing that can stop you or get in your way is you, so don't let it.

I will never forget Tom the custodian, Marvin the plane boarder, Brent the copy salesman, Amy the drive-through woman, Dave the poker dealer, and so many more. They will never be forgotten because it's not what you do that will get you remembered, it is how you do what you do that will sort your place in the history books.

We all know Abraham Lincoln, the 16th president of the United States, but few know the 21st president. We all know Martin Luther King, Jr., but few know the gentleman at his side in the famous Million Man March picture. We all know Babe Ruth, but not so many remember who batted before him even though they were on the same team in the same sport at the same time. Why? Simple. It is because we don't remember someone for their position or what they do. We remember them for how they did it. Do it legendary. Be legendary. It's that simple.

Left: Dr. Martin Luther King, Jr.
Right: Babe Ruth

So what I'm saying is, I do not care if you're a street sweeper, a landscaper, a coach, a president, an entrepreneur, a CEO, an athlete, an actor, an actress, a janitor, a fast-food employee, a politician, or a used car salesman. Whatever it is you do, it only matters how you do what you do. That being said, if you are miserable, you will never be in the state to perform to this level that we speak of. So, if you're miserable, we have to get you out of that state, and don't worry. We'll do that as well in this book.

That is why finding your passion, your calling, or your purpose is key to living your best life. This process might not be easy for some, and for others, you are probably already there. Like I said, it doesn't matter where you are in the process. The key is that you're in the process, and you're continuing to be in the process and growing into the best you and living your best life.

Throughout this book, we will go over some attributes that many legendary people have in common. I think the mixture of some of these skills are needed for all of us to be able to reach one's best life. I'm not saying you need them all or you have to be amazing at all of them. Just a mixture of some degree is key. You can see which ones you already possess and your strengths through them. Like many have said before me, after you identify your strengths, go all in on them.

The sun came up. You are reading this. You are breathing, and that means you have a chance. You have the opportunity to become a better you, no matter where you are along your transformation into becoming the best you. Like I say at the beginning of every daily conversation, if you're on the mat, if you're on the mountaintop, if you're climbing the ladder, or if you're just getting back on your feet … Welcome home. It's all fair here. It's all square.

I will tell you one of my many goals is to never see my masterpiece. What I mean by that is, one day I will not open my eyes, and I will leave this rental, also known as a body. That is when my masterpiece will be finished because I plan to keep growing into the best me till that day.

I want you to know there is no deadline on the best you. I don't care if you're 20 or if you're 80. I don't care if you're 16, like my daughter reading this, or 70, like my mom. Wherever you are, you can still grow. You can still become the best version living your best life for you.

There is no age requirement. There is no requirement of a bank account, of a position, of a power, or a career. I don't care what car you drive or what brand of clothes you wear, nice or not. No offense, it means nothing. All it means is where you are and where you want to go. If you know those two things, you're getting there.

I hope you enjoy this journey, and thank you so much for taking it with me. Let's get into the meat and potatoes of this thing. Welcome to Chapter 1.

Chapter 2

THICK SKIN

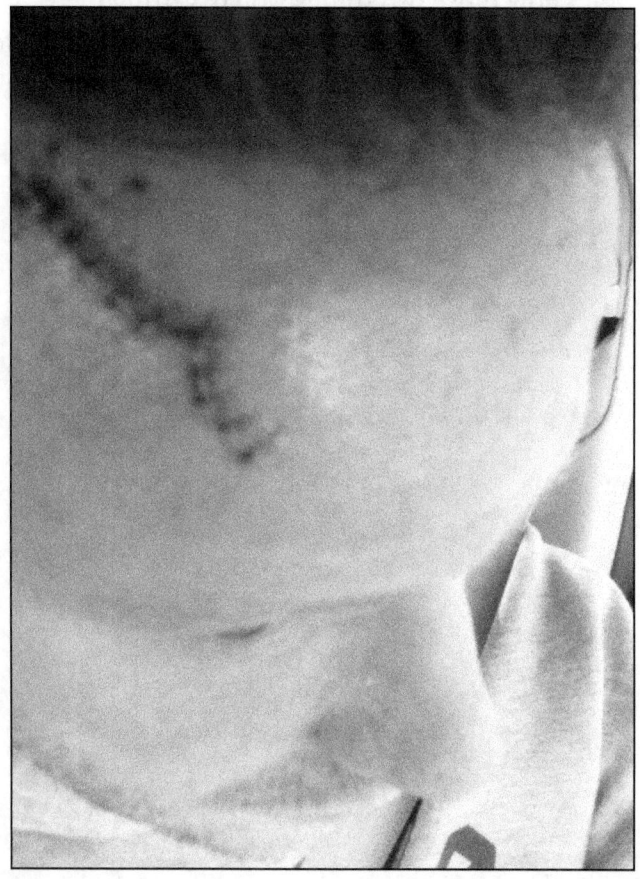

"Sing like no one's listening, love like you've never been hurt, dance like nobody's watching, and live like it's heaven on earth." – Unknown

I wanted to start here. I don't think we understand how important this is, especially in this climate, in this environment, and the way the world is right now. In the always offended, ultra-sensitive time that we live in, having thick skin now can be one of the biggest strengths of a personality to be successful that there could be. No, I'm not kidding. This isn't a joke.

I think this could be, if you were to ask me a question like, "What's the most important skill to have?" I might say, "The ability to have thick skin right now because it's so rare."

We get offended so easily. We get upset so easily. We almost get disconnected from our goal. We almost shut down and are so willing to quit at the first sign of adversity. If you are not that way, you are the kind of person that will keep going towards your goal and could block out what I like to call "the noise." So many are not capable of that now, and if you are capable of that, you have a heck of an advantage.

Listen, people are going to talk about you. I think that's a great place to start, to be able to block out what people say: "the noise." There are all different kinds of noise. There are people that really care about you that are going to try to protect you and tell you, "Don't take the risk," or "Don't go for it." They might say, "You do this really well," or "Just stick to this." It's all in good faith. They don't do it to hurt you, and they don't do it because they don't care about you or your dreams.

They do it because they probably love you, and they want to see you do well. They don't want to see you fail. They don't want to see you hurt, and they don't want to see you go through what the people are going to say about you and the struggles that you're going to deal with. The struggle is another one we'll talk about later in this book, but people are going to say things, including the people that care about you. Imagine what the people that don't care about you are going to say. People are going to make fun of you to your face and behind your back. People are going to make subliminal posts about you on social media (my personal favorite). Some others are not going to be so subliminal. They're going to come right at you.

The better you do and the more you do, the more they're going to come. Understand this, there's no level of success that stops people from trying to tear you down. The higher you go, the harder they'll hit the tower on which you stand on to try to knock you off of it. Some will want what you have. Others will hate that you have it. Either way, they're not going to be friendly about it. They're going to say mean things. They're going to do mean things. They're going to try to hurt your feelings. They're going to try to distract you.

I remember the movie in which Kevin Costner was pitching. Oh man, it was like the "perfect game." He kept saying, "Clear the mechanism." He blocked out the noise of the crowd, all of the people screaming, and all the other players. He was laser-focused on the catcher and where he wanted the ball to go, and that blocked out the noise. I always thought about that moment, and how we can use that in everything we do in life, in any profession you're in. You don't have to be a major league baseball pitcher to use that. Listen, I don't think I'm hugely successful. I don't think I'm on top of the leader board in any facet of life. I think I'm fighting to be. I think I'm moving up, but I'm very happy where I'm at. This isn't a poor me section. This isn't a great me section either.

This is me saying that even where I'm at, people are already saying things. I have people close to me saying things. I have people taking subliminal shots at me. People are going to say things, and Listen, if these guys think they have a chance to hurt my feelings, the things I went through when I was younger were much harder than what people are saying or doing now. This is coming from the guy that was born deaf. I didn't get the ability to hear until I was 3 years old. I didn't really know how to talk or read that well when I started school. I was made fun of all throughout lower and middle school.

In fifth grade, I had to go to third grade for reading classes. You don't think people said some jokes then? My middle school teacher literally brought my parents in and told them they should take me out of school to teach me a trade because I was so far behind (side note: thank you, Mom and Dad, for not listening to her). I was called dumb, stupid, and handicapped. I was called numerous things on a daily basis. They said I couldn't learn and was mentally disabled. I didn't know what that meant. They said I had ADHD, and there was a problem.

There is always an excuse. People said all kinds of things about me. They weren't exactly nice. Most of the time, they weren't nice at all. To be honest, I still think about those things and use those things to this very day as motivation. When I was in high school, I became a little rebellious. I became angry. I lost my brother when I was young, and that really changed my outlook on life. I lost another friend in high school, and I lost my pops as a teenager. I developed a "me against the world" mentality. I was upset and had a temper. Really, I was hurt, but no young man, especially in their teenage years, wants to say they're hurt because that isn't cool.

Mad is so much more masculine and strong, so I was mad. So, I did stupid things, and I got in trouble. I got into fights. I was more of a punk than most teenagers were. I remember someone that worked with the administration at one of the schools I was at, said that I would be dead or in jail by 21 years old, and they came close to being right.

I mean, I'm still human, so sometimes I get mad. I think about that and I go, "Yeah, let it go. Don't prove him right." Now listen, I'm way past 21 now. Good Lord, he wasn't right. Thank you. I still don't want that to be my destiny now. So rather than letting that anger make me do things that will cost me like I did when I was younger, now I make it work for me.

Now listen, any way you can get motivation, I'm not going to tell you it's bad. We'll talk about that later in this book as well. It can't be your only way. Because when you prove them wrong, what's next? Although it can't be the sole reason, it can be a way. The doubters, the naysayers, and the nonbelievers should push you a little bit. Anything you need and can use for motivation to keep your fire burning towards a goal or objective, I say, "More power to it." You're not going to hear me say, "Oh, that's negative motivation." No. If it's pushing you to get you better, I'm all about it. Use it.

I say the biggest thing, the biggest conversation, the biggest naysayer, and the biggest person to bring you down isn't anyone outside you. It's that voice in your head. I go around and give presentations to crowds of all sizes and ages. When I do, I always ask this question, "Who is the most important person you converse with every day?" You'll get all different answers.

You'll get "God or whatever they call God." You'll get "mom or dad."

You'll get "friends." You'll get "siblings." You'll get "grandparents, guardians, priests, or pastors." You'll get all these answers.

I always say, "No, no, no. That's important, yes but no. That's not the answer I'm looking for."

It isn't the answer because the most important conversation you have every day is with yourself. Self-talk is huge! So when you keep telling yourself in your head that you're bad, that you're not smart enough, and that you're not good enough, and when you keep putting these limiting beliefs on yourself and on what you can do, Well, of course, sooner or later, you're going to believe them.

When you believe negative self-talk, all that does is make you think that you can't achieve something, so why go for it? Why try? You know how many people I work with on a weekly basis where they have these great ideas, dreams, and goals?

They're like, "We really can't do them because this one time I messed this up, so You know I'm not smart enough for it."

I'm just like, "What?"

When you're a baby, you can barely walk. You can't, really. You have to learn how. The first time you attempt to walk, you probably fall, and then, you probably fall a dozen more times after that.

Heck, I still fall sometimes now, but it doesn't mean we stop walking. It doesn't mean we believe we only have seven steps, and then we have to fall down. Imagine what kind of life that would be if we just believed that what we did our first or second try was as best as we could get. Think about how many things you would have missed in your life. Any word you tried to say probably wasn't correct the first couple times you said it. It is as similar as walking or dancing. I imagine some of you still aren't able to do that (sorry, I had to joke about your dancing). I'm a pretty good dancer, just saying.

How many things did we have to learn? The only way to learn is by trying. Stop telling yourself all these negative things about yourself. Right? How many times has someone said (or someone reading this), "Oh, I can't believe I'm so stupid," or "I'm not good enough for that." How many times has someone said, "I'm not smart enough for this," or "I'm not talented enough to do that." How many people respond, "No, I can't do that. It's just not in me. It's not in the cards. I wasn't made for something like that. Everybody has their talents. That's just not mine."

I imagine every single person reading this at this point has done that. That's okay. Listen, I'm with you. I've done it numerous times, but the thing I started to do more recently is when I do something good, I say, "Hey, look at that. You're smart. Look at what you can do. Look what you've got." I don't do that for ego. I don't tell other people that. I'm not boasting. Ego is what you tell other people. Self-esteem is what you tell yourself. If you're going to recognize all the things you do wrong and tell yourself about them, the least you can do is tell yourself about the things you do right. That's the only way to balance the scales.

Let's not be sheepish here. Let's not be naive because we're all going to fail if we're trying to do anything worth a dang. I mean, really. Think about how many times people have failed. Think about how many times great people that have done amazing things still fail. The names can go on and on and on. Some names will be in this book. There is only enough room to mention some of those names. Hopefully, they'll make the next one. But, if you're doing anything extraordinary, you're going to fail trying it numerous times. There are people on record that have done amazing things that failed a thousand, two thousand, even ten thousand times. There are people that went bankrupt over and over again that have become billionaires or have become legendary and have moved the flag so much further down the field that they'll never be forgotten for their work. All of them have failed like all of us have.

There are people that if we just judged their life by one chapter of their story, we would think they were possibly the worst failures to ever exist, but in reality, they were huge successes. Huge success stories with huge triumph over tragedy are the best kind of stories and are the ones we want to read, and hopefully, like this one you're reading now. We're all going to fail. We're all going to mess up. We're all going to make mistakes, at least if you're doing anything worth a damn. Heck, I make them even when I'm not doing anything worth a damn. You know how many times I've burned toast? I'm sure everybody can relate to that. You know how many times I've spilled a drink?

Heck, when I was young, we used to have a calendar, and we'd mark the days that I didn't spill (thanks, Mom). It is sad but true that I spilled that often. I'm always very thankful for the life I had growing up. I had a mom that celebrated everything. I swear if I flushed the toilet, we were going to have cake later because of it, but, what she did was she made me see the good I did too. She made me get this higher belief in myself from before I can even remember. She wasn't just correcting me for the wrong but celebrating the little successes. Celebrate any victory!

I'll tell you from experience. Whatever goal I have set for myself, being able to celebrate the little victories and by doing so has made it so much easier to get more little victories. From trying to do different things like coaching sports and having a couple of businesses, it has lit the fire over and over again. It has kept me motivated and has kept me focused on the goal because when I achieve one, I want another one and another one. It doesn't stop. I have to thank my mom for that, for just really beating it into me that I could win. (whoa, not literally).

Maybe my dad but not her. Figuratively speaking, I mean

"beating" as in I'm going to screw up, but I'm also going to succeed and to celebrate the victories. I don't know if I ever told her thank you, but hopefully, she reads this and sees how much it meant to me. Also, we need thick skin when setbacks happen, when we do mess up, when we do fail, and like we talked about, when we fall short of the goal. Setbacks are going to occur.

Listen, the plane wasn't built the first try. The car wasn't successful the first try. We can go on and on about inventions that had setbacks and about people that had setbacks in life who still needed to find a way. Just because you have a setback, it doesn't mean that it's time to quit. It's not time to give up. It's not time to pack it in.

That is where the thick skin comes from. We have to take setbacks in stride. Listen, a setback is a learning opportunity; also, failure is a learning opportunity. We're going to get better. That's what we're going to do. I love some coaches, when they say, "When we lose we get better. When we win, we hide it." I love that because it's so true. It's when we mess up that we learn what to do differently, what to do better and how to improve. We get better by failure. We get better by setbacks. That's why it's not really that catastrophic when we have it. It's not that bad because we can learn from it. Growing and learning is the key. All of this will propel us into the future. All of this will make us better.

The key is to get at least a little bit better every day, maybe even much better but better is the key. We can't get better if we don't know where we can improve or know how to make it right. Just a little bit moves one from good to great and great to fantastic or phenomenal. Whatever it is, we want to keep moving it. Even if you're good, you can get better. Even if you're great, you can be better. There is this legendary mark I want us all to hit because we all can hit it. Heck, we are meant to be legendary.

That's the mark, and we're going to have to keep improving in order to get there. The only way we can do that is to fail and experience setbacks. It's almost like Will Smith said, "Fail great." Keep failing because you're going to keep learning. Failing is almost good, and in a way, it makes you know that you're trying something new and learning something new. That's the way to improve. So listen, if you failed, good job. Learn from it and keep going. You got this!

One of the hardest things to get across to clients is the whole fair idea. We're all looking for a fair shake. I want a fair hand. I want a fair deal. I want a fair game. How many times has anyone heard these? How many times have you heard this yourself? "That's just not fair." Well, Yeah. Let's get this deep secret that we all know already to get it out of the way: life's not fair. Life isn't going to be fair and rarely, anything is. It's not fair when you have setbacks. It's not fair when you fail. It's not fair when you lose people, businesses, or whatever it is. It's not fair. It's not fair when you have to go through certain things that you shouldn't have to go through. It's not going to be fair. I think you would rather go through thinking this won't be fair than thinking it will be and be disappointed from it.

So, now if you're saying this will not be fair and then if it comes out to a fair shake, Cool. Be joyous. Be thankful. Heck, be happy for it because we're not expecting it. Fair doesn't really exist. Fair is an expectation we set on something by feeling we deserved better. This isn't right. Who determined what's right? I'm not naive. Neither one of us should be. Most of us if not all of us will know someone that was stricken by cancer. That's never fair. You're never like, "You got that because you should have." At least, I hope not. It's not fair. People are suffering, working two jobs barely being able to make end meets. Men and women of the military are coming back and do not have a home or family to come to, and they are not getting the treatment they deserve. It's not fair. I know it's not, and you know it isn't. That is life though.

Fair doesn't exist. Fair is something we set. It's a level. It is a standard which we set for others, for events, or for times in our life or whatever it is. So if we stop thinking that anything is fair or everything is not fair, we accept it's all just life. So, if there is ever a situation where it's fair, be thankful. This isn't supposed to happen. I'm glad it did. It's nice. We have to change the way we look at it and think about it in order to make the setbacks, the failures, and the times where it isn't really fair less difficult to get through tough skin.

You need some thick skin to get through it, but you've got to start building it up. It's not going to be fair. You're going to fail. You're going to have setbacks. You're going to have some self-doubt, but tell yourself some of the good stuff too. People aren't going to say nice things about you all the time, even some of the people that really care and love you. They're not going to be rooting for you and pushing you. They're going to be saying, "Hey, it's okay. You're doing really great right where you are." That might be all true and well, but it's not where you want to be. It means you have to keep going no matter how much they try and protect you.

I feel like the last part of this chapter is the most important. Rejection comes. Rejection comes to us all. I remember when I was young and had this huge crush on this girl. I think her name was Renee. I thought she was beautiful. She was a couple years older than me. I think I was in middle school, and she might have been in high school. Man, I really thought I had a chance. I told you about the mom that I have that I'm so thankful for, and I'm sure I'll say that about a million times and how she celebrated all my successes. Man, she made me believe I was something special and that I could do anything. Sometimes that bit me in the butt. This is one of those times: so, I get this fake, pearl bracelet from Avon. I don't even know where I got it from. I might have actually stolen it from my sister. Who knows? (Elena, if you're missing that bracelet, it wasn't me, still. Sorry). I take this bracelet and find her outside the school; I pop it open, and I'm like, "This is for you because I love you, and we're meant to be together," like I had any idea what that kind of love was or what it meant. I don't even think I knew this girl's full name. I don't think I knew her favorite color. I didn't know her birthday (there was no Facebook to check). I'm sitting there saying, "We're meant to be together." Right? It's hilarious thinking about it now.

The rejection that came with it was just as equally hilarious now. It wasn't so hilarious then. I was devastated. I said, "Why wouldn't someone like someone like me?" I cried. I'm not a cute crier. I have red hair and fair skin. I get real red and welt easily in my face area almost every time I cry. At that age, I took crying as a weakness. It made me rageful because in my mind, I made believe this was the true love story of middle schoolers. I don't even think she was a middle schooler, but it was rejection.

It was one of the first times I remember being rejected, where I went all out for something, but I learned. It took some time, and I got over it, kind of. That pearl bracelet was really nice though. I thought that was for sure going to win her over, but rejection comes. It comes in many ways. It can come in every single type of way: personally, relationships, professionally, spiritually, or emotionally.

You can have all kinds of rejection, and you probably will in every area of life. That's okay. If you get everything you go for the first time or first couple times, you're not going for much. I remember going for numerous jobs I didn't get. I never went for a job I was qualified for. Why would I want that? I'm already qualified for it. I want the job I'm not qualified for. The only way I'm going to learn that job is by getting it. I'll never be qualified if I don't have experience, right?

Every job application says experience. Well, I can't get experience if I don't try. So, I'm going to experience some rejection, and it means I'm going for something bigger than which I have now. That's a good thing. That means you're on the right track, and the more you experience that and keep going forward, that's that thick skin we're talking about. Forget fair; find worth it.

I remember Rocky Balboa. "Life's not about how hard you can hit," he said. "It's about how hard you can get hit and keep moving forward." That's so true when we talk about thick skin. One person had more thick skin than I have ever known of or ever read about. That was Albert Einstein. Yeah, Einstein was a genius. Yes, he did amazing things . His creations and thoughts in science and just in life in general were amazing. What you didn't know was, or probably didn't know ...Well, I didn't know until doing some research for this book, Einstein didn't even speak until he was 4 years old. At 16, he failed to pass the test into the school he was trying to get in, the Swiss Federal Polytechnic School. While he did graduate, he struggled. He nearly dropped out and did very poorly in most of his coursework.

The truth is that when his father passed away, he was actually considered a major failure in his father's eyes which left Einstein heartbroken all the way through his life. He ended up actually taking an insurance salesman job. Einstein was an insurance salesman. He was

Albert Einstein

going door to door selling insurance. The guy that brought you the theory of relativity, can you believe that? Years later, he took a job as an assistant at a patent office and then, all of a sudden, things started clicking. Because of his amazing work in physics and mathematics, we now have knowledge about how the universe works.

The guy that won the Nobel Peace prize in 1921, was the same kid that was made fun of, called names, and made to believe he was stupid. We are talking about the same kid that couldn't talk until 4 years old, failed examinations to get into schools, and was made out to be a failure and a disappointment to his father until his father's dying day. The same man that won the Nobel Peace prize was a door to door insurance salesman (look it up).

Do you think if Albert Einstein listened to all the people that said negative things about him from when he was a young child all the way to young adulthood, even his father, he would have succeeded...? Do you think if he didn't have thick skin, if he didn't have full belief, and if he didn't understand that you're going to go through rejection, he would have kept trying? Do you think that if he didn't understand that life's not fair, if he didn't understand the setbacks, if he didn't understand failure or self-doubt, or what people were going to say and think about him, he would have persevered? If he couldn't get through all those things we talked about now, would he be able to do what he did?

No, of course not. Like so many say all the time, and you'll hear me say it a million times in this book, "If anyone can do it, everyone can do it." Albert Einstein isn't made of anything different than any of us. He isn't. Don't get me wrong. I might not win a Nobel Peace prize. I probably won't. I'm not really going for one either, but I know if he did it, then I could do it if I put my mind to it. If I made that my goal and if I dedicated myself to that, I could do it, just like you could. Any of us could because one of us did.

We're not born special. Every single one of us is born to do great things and to make this life better in our time. Every single one of us is made up of that greatness that we are here to accomplish. Albert Einstein showed it and so did many others. I'm hoping for the next book or the one after that, I'm writing your name down as the person that went through such adversity or tragedy, and you still found a way to let the world see your greatness (thick skin, you're going to need it).

Chapter 3

MIRROR, MIRROR

"Your time is limited, so don't waste it living someone else's life." – Steve Jobs

I called this chapter "Mirror, Mirror" because it's all about you, and you are the most important part of this equation. It has to be you. We're talking about you living your best life as the best version of yourself and about forgetting what everybody else thinks or says. We're talking about you focusing on what you feel and believe and what you know is your calling or your purpose. As cheesy and cliche as it sounds, you being good with yourself and having self-love, whatever term you want to use that you feel more comfortable using, is key. You have to love yourself. You have to be okay with yourself, where you are, where you've been, and where you're going. You have to be okay with all of this because if you're not, then you know you have to change it. There are some things we can't change. The first part of this is accepting your past because it is what it is. I think we all have a past that we've done things we wish we wouldn't have done. We haven't done some things we wanted to do or would have been best for us. We've made some mistakes. We have blemishes. We have scars. We have pains. We have hurts and regrets, and that's a painful word itself.

We have these things that are tough, things that make it hard to accept. It makes it difficult to embrace. We don't have to like our past. We have to accept it and not just the things we did but the things that we felt we were wronged on or things done to us that were just not right. Will Smith says something, and I love it. He says, "It might not be your fault, but it's damn sure your responsibility." I think about my past quite often and the people I've lost that I felt wronged in losing: losing my brother, losing my pops, and losing many dear friends in the last couple of years as well as when I was younger has made me have weaker moments. Of course I look, and I go, "Man, this isn't right. This is B.S. This is bogus."

For lack of a better term and I hate this term, "It is what it is." It has happened. It is there. What am I going to do with it? Am I going to fight it? Am I going to pretend like it didn't happen? Am I going to try to block that part out and never dive into that part of my life? No, I'm going to go through it and grow from it.

Winston Churchill said, "If you're going through hell, keep going." Some of the most painful moments, let me rephrase that, I've learned the most from the most painful moments. I'm never going to forget when my life changed in 2011 forever. One of my best friends, a gentleman I asked to be in my wedding party, passed away. He took his own life. You want to talk about a painful time? It hurt. There were many days I never wanted to even look at that or think about that part, but life has a funny way of making you. I figured out I had to go through it, or I'd never get past it. I would never learn to live with it. If I don't know how to live with it, I can't live the best life I can at the moment, whatever it is, and if I don't, I can't keep working towards living the best life I could live. I can't go towards my legacy.

I can't leave my imprint if I can't get to the point where I can make the impact to leave the imprint. It hurt when I lost him and still hurts to this day. I'm not over it. I've learned how to make that a part of my mission, my calling, and my purpose. It's part of my passion. That's why I don't need an alarm clock to get out of bed because I know what I'm doing, and the list can go on of people I lost along the way. I imagine all of us, including you reading this book right now, have suffered loss, defeat, setbacks, mistakes, failures, and all the things we talked about already in Chapter 1. Can you accept that part of your life? I'm not saying you have to smile when you think about it. I'm not saying you have to cheer because of the mistakes you made. You have to accept it. You can't let it keep you. That is the reason why it's holding you back. You have to be able to look in the mirror and say, "I'm good with where I'm at because I know where I'm going."

You know what you've been through and accepting your past is a huge part of getting to the future, heck, of getting into the present. You can't get stuck back there. We can't go further down the road looking in the rear view mirror, and if you do, it's very dangerous. Believe me, I've done it sometimes actually driving. It's not good for anybody, but in your life, it's not good for you. It's not good for the people around you and the people you're supposed to impact. Let's say if you're stuck in a bad relationship in your past, if you're stuck with thoughts of bad friendships, if you're stuck with thoughts of a bad business that you owned or worked for or whatever it might be, how can you fully embrace what you're in? If that's where you're stuck, you can't be all in where you're right now. You will create your own self-destructive prophecy where you're destroying yourself, and you're setting yourself up for failure.

If we don't learn to accept our past and embrace the challenges for what we've learned even with all the pain, even with all the scars, tears, and moments of just almost hatred towards ourselves, we will never grow. Whatever it was is in the past, that doesn't have to be your current situation, and that doesn't have to be your present. It has no right to be in control of your whole story, and that doesn't have to be your future. I remember the story. There's this kid, and he kept asking his grandfather about the perfect present. He kept trying to buy this perfect present all the way until his grandfather was passing away when he was an adult.

He said, "Grandfather, I never found the perfect present for you. I've been trying all these years. "His grandfather looked at him and said, "You always had it, including right now."

A perfect present is a gift, but it's not one you buy. It's one you embrace. It's now. This very moment is the perfect present and because you've gone through what you've gone through in the past that led you to this very moment, it doesn't mean it has to hold you in this moment.

It doesn't mean it has to hold you back from the next one. Your past is just that, the past. Learn from it and move on from it. The faster you do that, the better it is for you and the longer it takes for you to do that, the longer it takes you to get to the best life you can live. That's what we're all wanting. If you admitted it or not, we all want to live the best life we possibly can. I'm not saying it's full of riches, rainbows, unicorns, or lollipops. It might be. It might not be. Your best life is completely your vision. It's your artwork. It's your masterpiece. We'll talk about all this throughout this book, but we all want that. We can't get to it if shackles of yesterday are keeping us from tomorrow. Another part of the loving yourself is knowing your strengths and weaknesses. Listen, we're all human beings. None of us are perfect. None of us will have all strengths. Right? I have some friends that are like, "Oh no, I really do everything well." No, you don't. "I do everything excellent." No, you don't. Stop it.

I think so often we try to cover up and hide our weaknesses because we think that they will make it less like not everybody has them.

Like, "Oh, I can't let this guy know I'm weak at this because then he'll use that against me." Those people that are looking to use something against you don't care if you give it to them or not. They're going to use whatever means necessary, but by the time they are focused on you, you'll be focused on achieving your goals, you're leaving them in the dust. Listen, your goal should be to outgrow the you of today. It might not be to beat them, right? It's not to rub it in their face. It is nothing like that. It shouldn't really have anything to do with them. It might be motivation to get you where you want to go, but where you want to go is the key. By growing as a person, you're going to outgrow them. Listen, I'm sure right now you've outgrown some of your friends. Your friends aren't the same friends they were years ago. Or at least not the same way.

Some are and maybe some aren't. I would say almost definitely you're going to outgrow people, and that's okay. There's nothing wrong with that. I used to feel guilty like I talked about earlier when my friend passed away in 2011. His name was Mat Carter. He was a great, young man. A lot of the people I was friends with at that time, I barely know now. For so long, I felt guilty because I was going down this different path after his death. I felt guilty that I was leaving this group of friends that went through this tragedy. There's nothing to feel guilty about growing as a person. You see your strengths, and you see your weaknesses. We all have them. I'm not going to sit here and say work on your weaknesses. They're not that weak. No, no. I'm one of those different breeds that say double down, triple down, quadruple down, everything down, and go all in on your strengths. A bunch of other people say that now, but it used to be frowned upon. It used to be know your strengths, and that's fine but also work on your weaknesses.

Most of the things you're weak at, you really don't want to do. You're not really passionate about those things. You're not really thinking of flying a kite. (True story. I can't do it.) I don't know why. Between the wind and how to move it, I just can't figure it out, but I don't really find it interesting because I really don't want to do it or care about it. I don't want to fly a kite. Last time I flew a kite was because my daughter wanted me to. I wanted to make her happy. I'm passionate about that. Also, I feel like I'm good at it (at least better than flying a kite). I think that's one of my strengths, but most of the time, your weaknesses are something that you really don't care about and don't want to do. You're not passionate about it. It's not your purpose or your calling. Normally, things that are your calling, your purpose, your passion, or your pursuits are things that you're talented at because you were willing to master the craft. They are things you're pretty good at or even great at, but you have to know them. For example, if you want to be a professional basketball player, we know what you got to work on. Right? Let's say you want to be a lawyer, but you don't know how to debate. Well, you have to work on your debating skills. Even if you're weak or strong at it, you can do it. It just takes time. Nothing is instantaneous except the oatmeal. Well, now pretty much everything is instant in the microwave, but unfortunately, we haven't translated that to real life skill setting or achieving. We haven't said we believe that microwave is supposed to be part of our growth towards achievement, and it's just not true. It's not real. Let's say it takes 10,000 hours or more to master a craft. Tell me what you spent 10,000 hours mastering, sleeping? I'm pretty good at it. I mean, what, eating? What have you spent 10,000 hours to perfect, and if you don't name the things that you're passionate about and the things you feel like are your calling, then what are you doing? You know, I love being a success strategist. I love it.

It's actually the most fantastic thing. I love doing leadership trainings, team building trainings, and personal growth, personal development, self-care, and self-love trainings. I love it. I love doing speaking engagements. You can give me a microphone, and I'll rock a microphone. I'll rock the stage. Man, people standing up, will get applause, will get all kinds of stuff. I'm all about it. Part of this, this very thing actually, writing a book is something I'm not wild about. I don't love it. It's not one of my strengths. I'll tell you right now. Thank you for reading this, but if you think this is good, thank you. I'm humbled and honored by your opinion but come see me live. I promise on everything it will be better. This is what I do. My strength is I can do that. I can speak to you, and I can see you engaged. I can see the feeling and the emotion and also what's going on and what's important to you. At that moment, I know it's not about me. It's about you.

In this book, I can't do that. Writing this, speaking this right now, whichever part I'm doing, I can't gauge your emotion. I can't gauge your feelings. I don't know if this is hitting you at all or not. I don't know if this is making the impact I wanted to make, but I'm going to try over and over to make it, to make that impact. The key is this: this is part of doing what I love to do, so even though I don't think it's my strength, I've got to do it because it's part of what I love to do. Know your weaknesses and know your strengths. It's okay to have both. Hell, that's normal and it's expected. We tried to have this fake norm, right? "F the Norm" can stand for many things. "Fake" among others is one, but when you try to make this fake persona that you're perfect, you are setting yourself up for failure. We edit our photos and videos and use fake lighting, right? People have fake colored contacts for their eyes. You could put filters so your skin looks great.

You can do all these different things now to be fake and to be a fraud, but you are not authentically and truly being yourself. Don't get me wrong. Some of them are really fun. Some of them are awesome. Some of the attractions can keep people's attention longer, so hopefully, they can get the message. I get it. I'm not against it, but in a time where it's the biggest thing is to be fake, be real. Be the star. Be real. We all have problems. We all have weaknesses, and we all have strengths. We all have things we're really good at and things were not, and that's part of being you. I don't want you to be perfect. I really don't. I don't think that would be much fun at all. I want you to be yourself because you have gifts to give, and you have lessons to teach. You have people to reach, and if you're not yourself, you never will.

Part of this is really just about being honest, completely honest about where you are right now, not just about your strengths and weaknesses, and not just accepting your past and things that you've done that you're not proud of. The only way we can map out where we want to go is to have two spots on the map: both our destination and where we're starting from. If we have those two dots, well, then we can make the path. If we got those, we can still make the path, no matter how far it is or how short it is. We can make the path, but those two spots on the map must be able to meet. You have to be honest and be completely honest. I mean down to the millimeter honest. You have to be all out and forward about where you are, and there's no wrong spot. There's no poor me, or I'm just not good enough because of the spot.

My life isn't where I want it to be. Your life is right where it is. We use these things like, "Oh, I should be further along. I should be in this position. I should be. I could be. I would be." It doesn't mean anything. This is what matters. Where are you right now? Wherever that is, it's fine. It's the truth. Be completely honest. Where are you? I keep saying this for a reason it's important. Take a second and jot it down. Where are you? Where are you financially? Where are you with your relationships? Where are you with your professional career? Where are you with your emotional state? Where are you with your mental state? Where are you with your spiritual state? Where are you with your personal growth? How are you getting better? You want to level up. Well, you have to be capable of leveling up, but where are you with these things? I think about this quite a bit. I think about this once a week, once a month, and every six months, and I do a huge breakdown of my life.

Where am I spending the most time? Where am I giving the most energy? What's giving me the most back? No, that's not selfish.

People will be saying, "You give to the cause no matter what you get." That's ridiculous. That's like saying keep giving to a relationship even though if all the other person is doing is abusing you. That's silly. Don't do that. There's a great exercise. I can't think of the name of the person that I heard this from. I would love to give them credit. Hopefully, I can figure it out, but they said there are 100 hours in a week. That's your hours, right? It's not sleeping. It's not eating. It's not using the bathroom. Right? There are 100 hours that those necessities are not a part of in a week, and if you write down what you're spending those hours on, I can tell you what the percentages are of you being really good at them in life. For example, if you spend 42 hours at your job, you're 42% likely to be really good at your job.

You spend 10 hours on the phone, and you're 10% likely to be really good at whatever you're doing on your phone. That's not the point. The point is when you break down those hours is that what you want to be spending it on, the percentages of your hours? Is that really what you want to be known for being good at? This guy was really good at playing any app on your phone, right? One was the Clash Of Clans game for example. This guy was really good at social media. He was all over. He's a rock star. Is that what you want to be known for? If it is, cool. Keep doing that. If it's not, why are you doing it? Well, we have to be honest about the things we do, where we are, and where we want to go, but we have to be completely honest about it. There's a reason why I keep repeating this stuff because it's extremely important. I don't want you to glance over it and think it's just another piece. We're getting into it. We're starting to get into the you part, so you are able to have the strength to leave the impact that you desire. That will be your legacy.

Wherever you are, whatever you're going to do, I want us all to feel it. The only way I can is by you being honest about where you are so we know how to get to where you want to go. That's the next key part. Where do you want to go? It's funny. I had this reoccurring dream when I'm awake, and I'm standing in this arena in Philadelphia. It's huge. Every seat is packed even the ones on the floor. There's this beautiful stage in the center, and then there are all these chairs. Even the seats in the stadium are just filled with people, and I'm the closing keynote speaker. I go last. Man, I rally the troops. I bring it home. I hit the home run. I'm cleanup and that's a big thing. It's a really big thing in the speaking world and in the coaching world. I see this picture over and over and over again, and I smell the air and what it feels like in there; I feel the heat of all the bodies in there.

They're just as excited to be there and to hear, learn, grow, and celebrate together. I feel the sweat on my forehead and the annoying feeling of the wireless microphone strapped around my ear, pushing on my skull. It's an annoying feeling by the way. Right before I go on stage, I feel that excitement, that adrenaline, and that energy. I feel it all. It gives me goosebumps just thinking about it. My hair is literally standing on my arm just talking about it, writing this right now. I do this every day. I can see the water bottle I'm holding before I go onstage. I see the crew, the UnleashU fam, all around me saying, "You got this brother."

We're giving our daps and hugs before I go onstage. I see how I jog out there. I do my normal, "What's up everyone?"

I see that all the time. Why? Because that's where I want to go. Man, I vision it, everything from what sneakers I have on to what I am wearing. How's my hair? How's my hair falling today? Hopefully, not out. It's already doing that at a record pace, but I see this.

I feel it, and I think about it every day, multiple times a day. It's not just that. That's one of my visions. Man, I see my visions about my family all around a Christmas tree, and there are presents everywhere. There are kids laughing and dancing just having a great time. I see all these things. I vision everything. I see everything where I want it to go and how I want it to be. I just keep working towards that, but I see it. You have to see it already. Listen, human beings are tangible animals. We have to be able to see the prize in order to get the prize. If you keep saying, "Well, I want to get this…" If you don't know what it looks like, how do you know what you really want or when you really get it? You want a car you've never seen? No. No one does. Do you want a house you've never seen? No.

I mean listen, maybe when I was young and out of my parent's house at like 16, yeah, sure I would have taken anywhere, but now you're crazy if you're like, "Hey dude, you can buy this house, but you never can see until you get it."

"I don't want it. No, thank you."

But then when we say you must be able to see your goals and dreams and wherever you want to get to, to your mountain top, we think, "Nah, that's not important."

Of course that's important. You have to see what you want. All of this adds up into this great idea of falling in love with the transformation of you: where you've been, where you are, and where you're going. Wow, look at that, another crazy tie up. Accepting your past, seeing your strengths and weaknesses, being completely honest about where you are right now, and seeing where you want to go, can all get torn and put together in this great idea of falling in love with the transformation of you.

It is a process. It is going to take time. It's going to take effort. There are going to be good days and bad days. There are going to be some painful ones, some happy ones, and some joyful ones. You're going to fill your cup over someday, and you're going to feel like it's dry the next. There are going to be a whole bunch of feelings and emotions and a whole lot of memories. That's the amazing part, but you're going to become the person you want to be: the best version of you living the best life you can live. When I sat here and was thinking about this chapter, I was really into this because this is so important, and I love this piece because the impact it had on my life and lives of people that are clients of mine big and small. It was easy who I was going to use. The person of this chapter is Charlie Chaplin. Charlie Chaplin probably is the greatest ever silent film actor.

Most people don't know he was born into poverty or that his father abandoned him and his family when he was around 2 years old, leaving his mom and this kid with no income really. At the age of 7, Chaplin had to go work in a workhouse to provide financial support: that 'is where the poorest people of a parish would go or were sent to to work for food, room and board, and other necessities. When he came back, his mom was committed to a mental asylum. He was 9 years old. He had to go back to the workhouse. How painful that had to be then? At 9 years old, you don't just have a mental breakdown from all this? Around that same time, his father who was extremely into the use of different types of drugs, including one being alcohol, passed away. Charlie was only 10 years old. A couple of years after that, his mother was back battling mental illness and was committed to asylum where she stayed until her death. His brother and he were pretty much on their own.

Charlie Chaplin

They went without food for days and survived. During this time, he was in some plays, and he really tried to perfect his comedic talents and his ability to dance. You all saw him step dance. He ended up in Hollywood, California. The best part was when he got there, he got turned away and ignored for parts. No one thought he was good enough. They didn't think he would be funny. They didn't think people would relate to him. They didn't think people would find him humorous or that the audience would enjoy him. He then turns around and becomes the biggest and greatest silent film actor that has ever blessed the stage. Think about going through all of that and still going. Think about being able to look in the mirror that he did every day knowing everything he battled and everything in his past that he had to accept; his mom was stuck in the insane asylum, and his dad left them with no money or anything. Charlie was forced to the workhouse multiple times at a young age. Then, when he finally thought he found his dream; instead, he is laughed at and told, "Get out of here because you're not any good."

Think about the transformation he went through. Think about how many times he visualized living that dream. I imagine it was a lot, but he knew his strengths and weaknesses just like we talked about in the last chapter. If anyone can, everyone can. Charlie Chaplin did it. I plead with you. Then accept your past wholeheartedly: the good, the bad, and the ugly of it. Find your strengths and your weaknesses. Embrace them. They're you. Be completely honest with yourself about where you are, what you've been through, what you can and can't do as of right now, and where you want to go, so you know what you have to fix. Fall in love with the process of transforming the person you see in the mirror every time you look at it. You can call this self-love. You can call this self-care. You can call this whatever you want, but this is crucial for you to live your best life as the best you. That's all I want for you.

Chapter 4

#SQUAD GOALS

"When my circle got smaller, my vision got clearer. There's strength in loyalty, not numbers." – Trent Shelton

I talk about this quite a bit if you follow me on any of my social media, my shameless plug? Look for the Coach Mike Fabber page pretty much anywhere on social media, and you'll probably find me.

We put content out there, at least I try to put content out there between quotes, little short talks, podcasts, short videos, and long videos when I'm giving presentations. I also put pictures of different leadership groups that I've been part of, and the list goes on.

One of the things I talk about quite a bit on there in all those ways is your inner circle. I think we forget how important our inner circle is. It is extremely important because now it's that whole image like I did it on my own, and no one ever helped me. The idea that I had to do all of this, and no one had my back, right? Have you seen this? Heck, have you felt or even did this? I think we think that adds to the story if we say that and act like that somewhere along the line someone will think it was actually true, and that I was a success story all by myself.

This is very far from the truth. You'll hear most of the people that make it do this. Do you know why they give thank-you speeches after winning awards? It is because there are people to thank because people help us along the way. Those people, some are just giving opportunities in business or life, but others are your inner circle. We all need that inner circle to help us get as far as we can, and know this, you'll never go further than the talent of your inner circle than the loyalty and love within it.

I just had this recent post about how your inner circle should be the ones clapping the loudest for you, and if they're not, you need a new circle. The importance of the circle is easy; you'll become like the people you surround yourself with, and they'll become like you.

I forgot who said the great quote: "Show me five people, if four are millionaires, I'll tell you who the fifth will be. Show me five people, if four are jerks, I'll show you who the fifth will be."

That's how important your squad is, no matter what you call it, your inner circle, your team, your crew, or your family. I've called it different names as I grew up myself. I imagine you probably have too.

Your family can be part of it, but they don't have to be. I say you want three things from the people around you: you want people that will build you up, people that will lift you up, and people that will check you to keep you up. Those are the three types of people that you want in your circle: they'll build you up; they'll lift you up, and they'll check you to keep you up. If you have that, you are covered.

For my inner circle, I want people to want us to do amazing things, that believe we're going to achieve great things, and that will do their part and more to be able to do those amazing things. They'll have each other's back when things don't go well because things won't go well all the time. We've already talked about it, and we will a little more. There are going to be hard days. There are going to be days you feel like you didn't win. There are going to be days that didn't go your way, and you feel like you didn't get closer to your mountain top. There are going to be tears, and there are going to be triumphs. I want people that are going to be there for both.

The love is unwavering. The loyalty is unwavering. We have to drop our shield, that protection we try to use, so we won't let anyone get close to us. A lot of times we won't do that because we think that we are protecting ourselves. We don't look at it as we're limiting ourselves. Think about the people that are closest to you…if you call me your brother and say, "I love you," but let's say I keep you at this distance because I don't trust you. What kind of life is that? What kind of team is that? What kind of squad is that? How far do you think you'll get living that way?

I'll be honest, with my squad, with my inner circle, and with my team, I'm very vulnerable. I put out there how I feel. I'm very truthful with them, knowing that they can turn around and use that against me, knowing that they can make fun of me for it, and knowing that they could bash me for it. It doesn't matter because if they do then I know they're not supposed to be in that circle, but your inner circle is key for you to get as far as you can get in whatever you want to reach.

Well then, if your goal is to be the best family man on earth, the man or woman you marry is key, and how you raise your children is key. The situations, the environments, and the culture you want to put them in is key. The people you surround them with is key to be able to achieve that because saying, "I really want to do this, but I'm going to go to these places where they teach them how to judge and make them feel better than other people" wouldn't make sense. Neither does saying, "I really want to be this amazing family man, but I choose a partner that's not dedicated to family, that's out partying all the time, and that's never home." What kind of family do you think you're raising? Do you think this is going to be the most amazing family?

I'm being honest here. Whatever it is that you have as these goals, the people you surround those goals with is critical to if you achieve them or not. Your inner circle will determine much of that. I think Les Brown said it correctly when he said, "You'll never outgrow your inner circle. You'll never go beyond their capabilities. That's how important it is. You'll never go past their capabilities. I'll never go further than them."

When I was young I used to hang out with everybody. I did. I had a clique. I had a crew, but I would hang out with anybody. It didn't matter to me. My dad would always tell me, "The people you hang around with are going to add to your reputation, like it or not, fair or not. If you hang out with four troublemakers, they'll think you're the fifth." And I didn't get it. Then I got in some trouble…

A couple guys that I hung out with got arrested. I couldn't believe how right my dad was. What did they do? They told the cops it was really all me and that I did everything. I had to spend years in court proving that I wasn't even part of what they said I was and that they completely lied, which they did. They completely lied about me, the people that I thought were my boys, my team, and my family, those that I literally got in fights for and would sacrifice for who wouldn't do the same for me. I never believed that until I was in that reality.

Unfortunately, my dad passed away before the whole ordeal ended, and I never got to tell him how right he was and that I learned that lesson the hard way. I've taken that lesson with me pretty much every step of my life since then. That's how important your squad is. If your goal is that important, your crew is even more important because they'll help you get to it, or they'll keep you from getting to it.

So, knowing who your crew is and choosing who's in it is important. Whew, that's the key. So choose wisely, and that doesn't mean blame them. They didn't get there by chance. You pick them!

My biggest advice for choosing your crew would be not to settle. Do not just accept someone in your crew because they're around. Don't just accept someone in your crew because you really don't see any better options right now: this is a convenient crew. I love, I always love when people I know say, "Oh man, there's this really good friend I work with. He's an awesome guy."

I'm like, "Oh, cool. What's up? Nice to meet you." That friend will get a new job. Two months later, I never hear about that dude again, and I meet another awesome dude that he works with and tell them, "That's a friend of convenience."

Don't get me wrong, there's nothing wrong with that, but if that's how you're picking your crew, out of convenience, I can tell you how the story goes. I can tell you the ending. Your results won't be because of hard work. Your results won't be because of the dedication, because of the sacrifice, or because of the struggle. You're willing to go through it. You will ask yourself, "How convenient was it?" You will get the same result every time.

So I heed a warning again, choose wisely who you put in your crew, and listen, you might pick the wrong choice. I have. I already told you one story. I could tell you multiple stories of where I picked the wrong people to be in my crew, to be in my squad, and to be in my family. You learn to recognize it. Admit it and then keep moving. Keep moving forward.

The phrase "addition by subtraction" is real. If they're not what they need to be for the family to get where it needs to be, then they're not part of the family because if they're not willing to do their part they shouldn't be a part of it. No, I'm not trying to be mean, and I know that sounds rude. You might be thinking, "Wow, this guy is just like, move on." If you're serious about living the life you want and if you're serious about living the best life for the best version of you and achieving these goals that should be beyond the moon, that's how important the people you put around you are.

When you sit back you have to notice and think about the friends you have or family you have. There's a reason why when you're in AA or in recovery people will tell you about "people, places, and things." If you change the people, change the places you go, and change the things you do, your life will change. Why would they say that? That's how important the people you surround yourself with are. That's how key they are in your life.

I know we try to act like no matter what's happening, you'll make it. I know we try to act like the surroundings, the people around us, the environment, and the culture have no impact, but it's what we see and it's what we hear every day.

This is how real this is. They took two plants and put them in the exact same conditions; there was one difference. One had positive phrases said to it all day, and the other one had negative phrases said to it all day. One was told, "You are good enough. You are beautiful. You are so smart. You are gorgeous." The other plant was told, "You are stupid. You are worthless." How crazy is that? The plant that was told the positive quotes thrived in the same exact conditions. It grew better, healthier, taller, and fuller than the one with the negative quotes, and that's a plant. Think about how we are. If we have people around us talking and acting negatively, that's going to make an impact on you. That's going to wear on you, and I bet you've caught yourself in these situations before. Heck, probably currently.

How many of us have sat around the table with our parents and listened to them talk about politics? It never fails. A couple days later, a political conversation comes up, and I'm saying the same thing they were since I am young. How many of us when we were growing up voted the same way our parents would or did? Why is that? Maybe it's because of the impact our circle had on us. Normally, when you're young your circle consists of your parents, grandparents, brothers, sisters, maybe some friends from the neighborhood, or maybe some of the local community guys. And that's your crew. You'll do a lot of things like they do, and you'll say a lot of things like they do. You'll act a lot of the ways that they do. That doesn't change. We're influenced by the people around us, and that's how important picking our crew or squad is. And that's why you cannot settle when you're doing it.

The other thing we have to be willing to do is learn from others. I recently went to this John Maxwell training. I'm a certified John Maxwell speaker and coach. It was a fantastic training. I recommend it to anybody and everybody. It was great. One, it's in Orlando and it's sunny. It's nice. The place is beautiful. There is everything you could want there, and it's very close to all the Disney parks. It's like 12 hours a day for those days you're in the convention and this conference.

They did this exercise where they gave you this piece of paper, and there are numbers 1 through 88 on it. So one, two, three, four, five, six, all the way up to 88, and they said, "All right, take this paper, go in order, 1 to 88. You have 30 seconds, start and see how far you can get." And you know, one will normally get to 11 through 15.

He then said, "What if I could tell you this…? I bet I could double your score."

Everybody's like, "What?"

And he continues, "I bet I could double your score, giving you one piece of advice in ten seconds. The one piece of knowledge that I have I can give it to you. You'll probably finish it in 10 seconds or less, and I'll give you another 30 seconds; you'll probably double your score or better."

You're kind of skeptical, and everybody's kinda like, "No way."

So, he says he will prove it, and he keeps going, "There's a line on the top and bottom, on each side. You can fold that, and it makes it into fours. And those are quadrants. And it starts top left, and it goes one and top right, two, bottom right, three, bottom, and left, four. It just continues going that way, five, six, seven, eight. So the number you are looking for now, rather than having to look at this whole sheet of paper is cut down into quadrants. So, there are four sections, and it's in that section and just keeps going in that order. And it never fails, everybody doubles their score.

The key to this exercise isn't to brag about what the guy knew: it's about being willing to teach, being willing to reach, and being willing to listen. Being willing to share and receive are huge in being able to get as far as we can get together. Think, if that guy had told us at the beginning of it, he would've saved me 30 seconds of wasted time and also frustration because I was actually getting pissed from not moving as fast I thought I should. Like, word searches are my thing. I couldn't find those numbers. If he'd just told me that, I would've raced through it at the first 30 seconds.

But the purpose is to understand that we can learn from one another, and we have to because there's no point in having a squad and making the same mistakes that the other person made in it when we know we don't have to do it. Now that's not saying set limits because of what they say, and that's not what I'm saying. If someone's telling you that in your crew, find a new crew member or a new crew period, if they believe it.

What I'm saying is we all have skills. We all have talents. We all have these gifts. It's our job to give them. It's also our job to receive them. I used to be a very prideful person. Some would say I still am but I'm working on it. I remember people used to offer things to me and offer to do things to offer help, and for a while I was like, "No, I can do it myself. I can do it all myself."

So for the last couple months, I've really been trying to work on that, because someone said this to me, "Why are you rejecting their gift? If God or whatever you call it gave them this gift and this is how they can use some of it or be able to give it back to the world, who are you to reject them from giving that gift?" I never looked at it that way. That was their part. That was what they were supposed to be giving, and I was rejecting them from giving it. I never thought how it made them feel or how it impacted their life. Don't reject gifts. Don't reject knowledge. Don't reject being able to learn from others.

That's how the crew pushes itself further… That's how we can save time. I would've saved that 30 seconds plus some. I would've saved the 30 seconds after when I was beating myself up saying, "I should've done better." That would've been a minute of time; also, I would've saved myself from all the negative thoughts I was saying about myself because of that exercise, if that person said at the beginning, "Listen, this is an easier way of doing it. Maybe this way will help you. I did it once, so maybe this will help you do better at it."

I think about how many times my parents said something to me that was 100% accurate, and I kind of avoided it and kind of ignored what they said and their warning and their advice. And then, Boom! It was right. I'm sure many of you can relate. One of the biggest regrets I have is not being able to tell my dad how right he was about almost everything he told me except that he could beat me in basketball. That wasn't right.

Seriously, I just sit here and think, "Man, how many times did he tell me and teach me, and I had to ignore it and find out for myself?" I also think about the time I would've saved and the agony I would've saved, where I would've been faster if I just listened and learned. We have to be willing to learn from each other before we make the mistakes and not after the mistakes are made like I have.

I'll tell you about my mom and dad. One of the biggest things I learned from them was that not everybody grows at the same speed. For example, I was young. There was me and another basketball player that were in middle school, but they wanted us to play on the high school team. And when I first heard of that, I wasn't very excited about it. I don't know, it might have been nerves. It might have been fear. What would happen if I had play on the high school team? The excuse I used was that all my friends were playing middle school basketball. So why would I not want to do that? How was it right for me to change teams and not them? That's not fair. We should have all got to do it, or none of us should have gone. That was my mindset. The other guy was named Tommy, who is still one of my friends. That big man saved me from a lot of beatings. I always appreciated him. So Tommy, if you're reading this, thank you. You saved some of my teeth and also taught me a lot about growing up which I'll always appreciate.

So when we were having this talk, my mom and dad just sat across from me listening to me talk about how it's not fair if I leave them and this middle school team. I think I was talking for probably 10 minutes, but it felt like for a lifetime; my dad just looked at me and said, "Son, not everybody grows together." I had no idea what that meant. I was just lost at those words. He said, "Not everyone grows together. We grow at different speeds. We grow at different times, and it's not right for any of us to hold others back from growing or from growing how each of us has to grow. It's not right to stay back for others to feel all right, and they should want you to." He said, "A lot of your friends are on the middle school team who won't like the fact that you turned down that opportunity. They'll be proud of you. You're a part of them, and you made it there. And then you might actually motivate them to do the exact thing that you do and sit out there for hours just shooting hoops."

I listened to everything they said, and I still thought it was a bad idea. Remember what I told you. It was a lot of the fear talking. But we both said our peace and as great parents do, they made the decision for me; I was playing high school basketball in middle school.

This is not to brag about my basketball ability; believe me, it's not very good, but it was one of the first times that I learned that we're not all going to grow together, and that you can't hold yourself back for others and the amount of people you can impact because you're trying to stay at the same speed as someone else. You're going to outgrow people, especially if you're working on yourself, your personal development and growth, or self-love and self-care. If you're really working on those things and people around you aren't, you're probably going to outgrow them.

We're not all meant to walk every step together. You know, they say, "People come in your life for a reason, or a season, or a lifetime." When I first heard that I always laughed at it and thought it was kind of ridiculous. The more and more I grow, the more and more I think that has some merit to it.

One of my best friends growing up, his name was Michael. I love him and still to this very day. Every once in a while I'll text him and just say, "Hey, I love ya, bro." He lives on the other side of the country. Our lives grew in different directions. They didn't grow at the same pace or place, and they didn't grow together. That doesn't change that he's my boy, and that doesn't change that he's my brother. That doesn't change the love I have for him and how I'm rooting for him. He's still part of my inner circle. He's just not right next to me. But listen, when he succeeds, when he triumphs, when he hits one of those achievement stones, I bet he hears my clapping from the other side of the country.

You're not all going to grow together. It's not going to be at the same pace. It's not going to be the same steps, and some things aren't going to be even near each other. And that's okay. That's part of it. You're going to outgrow people and situations. You're going to go in different directions. It's part of life. You've done it before, and you'll do it again. And it's okay. The growth is key. Don't stunt yours to try to stay with others. If you do, you hurt them and yourself.

Now this leads into a tricky part. This is a tricky one but very key. You have to really eliminate the toxic things. Now I'll tell you, when I was growing as a person, there were people I hung around that didn't want to grow. They didn't care to grow. It meant nothing to them. They liked what they were doing, where they lived, the jobs they had, the cars they had, the people they had around them, the culture, the environment, the things they were doing, and the impact they were making. All of it was fine. They didn't need any more and didn't want any more. There is nothing wrong with that. Nothing at all. If that's your best life, and that's the best you that you see or want or desire, you're living that best life. I'm proud of you. Cheers. I'll buy you a round. That's awesome. I strive for that so I get it.

The people that will come to you and say the "good enough" crap, that's not the life for me. Those people that bring toxins into your life by negativity, by holding you down, and by bringing those things in your life that can change your life forever, for the worst.

I sit and think about the friends I lost along the way, and who made the impact in their life that made them go down such negative roads? I think wow I wish I was closer to stop it and change it, so I could tell them they didn't have to do that. I wish I could have shown them that's not the road they should have been on when they were not living their best lives. They should have been and could have been more.

I think about my boy, Wig. I think about my boy, Ferris. They both passed away the last couple years from drug addiction. And I think, all they had to offer this world and when did they ever believe that was the best way for them? You have to keep the toxic away from you. I lost numerous people because of toxic. Now don't get me wrong, they're responsible for their choices. I get it. I'm not saying they weren't. We control our choices, but your squad should be there to help and not hurt. Keep the toxins out of your crew. Eliminate the bad. Be choosy. Be picky. Protect yourself. Protect the people you care about. You'll go as far as your crew. Don't be the reason why your crew doesn't make it as far, and don't let anyone in your crew that won't let your team make it as far as it can.

Most of this chapter has been talking about the people you allow around you, that you bring around you, and that you embrace around you. You are the key part in all that. I keep saying it because you have to do your part as well. What makes you good for the crew? Your circle? Your family? What value do you add? What value do you bring? Do you lead by that example? When people want you in their crew, their squad, or their family, always check yourself first. Make sure you are worthy of these gifts. Make sure you are where you need to be, to be able to help people around you. Make sure you are an asset to the crew and not the one bringing them down.

And listen, if you're like, "Oh man, maybe I'm not adding all I want," or "Am I adding anything?" It's not too late to start adding stuff. Start adding value right now. And listen, if you have no money, it doesn't matter. Have value. Be positive. Be one of the best cheerleaders in the crew. It takes no money for that; it just takes a little time and effort. Right? Be willing to be there. It takes no money. Be open and honest with them. It takes no money. It's not about money. You can add value without adding dollar signs. Make sure you're adding value.

As you can tell by my social media feeds, I wanted to stress the importance of a crew. When I was trying to think of a person I could use as an example to show the importance of your crew, your squad, and your family, one name kept popping up: Jack Canfield. If you don't know who he is, he's one of the creators and the contributors to the *Chicken Soup For The Soul* series. If you ever have time or just want to look him up, he is also a great motivational speaker. Now don't get me wrong. This guy was Harvard educated and is pretty smart and intelligent. He could probably write his own book. He probably didn't need to use a co-creator but he did. He chose Mark Hanson to be a co-creator with him and part of his crew. They put together the series, and you know, they got rejections.

Jack Canfield
Image courtesy of Derek Smith

They got rejected and the book got rejected over 140 times. One of the publishers went so far saying they wouldn't even sell 20,000 copies. You know, that same book has sold over 500 million copies.

They got this small-time publisher, that no one ever really heard of, who was willing to join the crew and be part of the movement. He wanted to be a part of the vision in which they saw, and they published the book. And do you think, if he didn't get this co-author, if he got a weaker co-author, if he never found the small-time publisher that was willing to join, if he never got these people in his crew, he would have been able to handle that kind of rejection? I don't know. I don't know if he would, but we don't have to know. Because he had the crew, he had the squad, he had the team, and he had the family, whatever you want to call it, around him to keep them going even through all of it. After over a year of rejection on the same thing and on the same project, he had a strong enough crew to say, "We're going to keep going because this is going to happen." That's how important your squad is.

So let me ask you a question. Is your squad that strong?

Chapter 5

IT'S YOUR CALLING ... ANSWER IT

"The Mastery of human existence lies not in just staying alive, but in finding something to live for." – *Fyodor Dostoyevsky*

It's like if the telephone keeps ringing, at some point you're going to answer it, turn it off or smash it.

We have all been in that position when the phone just keeps ringing. Now if a cell phone just keeps vibrating in your pocket, sooner or later, you're going to answer it. Why is it any different with our calling in life?

I'm sure I can speak for the higher percent that many of us feel that we are here for something bigger than we are doing or here for a greater moment than this one. That something we might not be able to point a finger at right now, but we know it's there. Some of us know exactly what it is, and some do not. It's our calling. It's your purpose. Some of you guys might be like, "Yeah, I just don't know what it is."

Well, then I ask a simple question: what are you passionate about? What's your gift? I ask that with this in mind. We know there are going to be some long days and some hard ones too. Those days that straight up suck! We know that we are going to have to sacrifice, and we're going to go through struggles. We know we are going to have rejection in life and the more we do, the more rejection will come. We are going to know we're going to get less sleep. We have to know that there are going to be taxing days and nights. There's going to be self-doubt and harsh, self-talk. There will be all these things that will deter us from doing this, whatever it is, no matter what you want to call it.

So I ask what your passion is because if I know I have to go through all that bad, if I know I have to go through all that tough crap, if I know I have to battle this struggle sometimes multiple times a day or for a period of time, I have to battle the struggle. If I know that, then to be able to get through it, I know it has to be something that I really, truly care about, and that I'm motivated on the inside to get through the outside. It all starts inside you to grow through the outside stuff. I don't need outside motivation; that stuff wears off. That inside motivation is what keeps you going. That's called passion. I have a passion for it, but do you have it for what you are doing?

Some would say I work long hours. Some would say I don't work enough. It depends who you ask, but I get out of bed every day, not because of my alarm clock, that might wake me up, but I get out of bed because I'm passionate about what I'm doing. I want to do it. I'm excited about it. I'm eager. I'm dedicated because I care. If you are not doing something you don't care about, how much are you going to give to it? How far are you going to get in it? How much of that struggle are you willing to take, or even more importantly, how much will you fight through if it means little to you?

There's a reason why people change careers every couple of years. It's because they get to the point where it's not worth the struggle anymore. They have put in enough time and energy that they are going to put into something like that. And listen, they're not the ones that I get worked up over. The ones that straight break my heart are the ones that I know put in 25 years for something they didn't care about that meant nothing to them, just so they can get some kind of retirement, and normally with their retirement, they can't really retire when they want. They still have to work another job just to make ends meet. So they dedicated 25 to 30 years to something that still wasn't enough, and they really didn't even care about it. What kind of life is that? What kind of impact did that person make? It is a shame!

So, I always start with your passion. We're going to take your passion and make it your purpose. I know that sounds super easy, but I also want you to know I know it isn't. There are a lot of things I'm passionate about. I had to figure out what I was the most passionate about. I had to dive deep inside myself to know what I really wanted to do on this earth and how I could do it. I have these buddies I know that spent hours making beer. I mean what better way to spend time on the stuff that some people like to drink here and there. They created different flavored beers. They have the whole process down. They've spent hours doing it every week and sometimes every day.

I'm like, "Hey, man, you ever think about selling that?"

"No, no, no, no, no, no. We're just messing around with it. I just like to do it. I just love doing it, so I just do it."

Why is it so crazy to turn something you love doing into your purpose, passion, calling, or career? Listen, there are probably hundreds, if not thousands, if not millions of people out there that like doing the same exact thing, and they might love what you're doing. You might motivate them to do their own thing rather than having a bunch of guys in basements somewhere making beer that only they get to try. What's the point of being passionate about something and not letting the world taste your passion? That's like if Leonardo da Vinci painted the Mona Lisa and kept it in his closet, and he didn't want anyone to see it. That's like if Michelangelo made the Sistine Chapel his private office rather than somewhere where people can go in and just see his passion, see his art, and see what he cared about and be moved by it. Why hide your art or your masterpiece?

Our gift isn't just for us. Our gift is for others to experience, and that's your passion. Let other people see it. Forget the judging part. Forget all the fear of what they might say and forget falling straight on your face. It happens anyway. I'm sure we all have if we tried or not. So there's no point. There's no benefit of taking something that you can leave an impact on others with and hiding it and keeping it for yourself. You empower others by being willing to share your calling.

You might be asking where do I start. This all sounds great to find your passion, all right, what's my passion? How do I start? Great question. It is an important question. This one is easy, and Simon Sinek perfected it. It's called your "why." Why is it your passion? Why is it important to you? Why do you care about it? Why does it drive you? You start figuring out why you're so involved in this. It's not easy. This is another tough thing, but it's the most important part of your life ... Your why!

I heard this once, I've actually heard it multiple times, where someone said, "I think it was the seven depths of why." It's in another book as well, *Success Habits of Millionaires* by Dean Grazioso. It's seven levels of why. So when you say your first answer, it's going to be something that your mind' has registered. Your second answer will probably be the same way, just a little more in depth or detailed. Your third one will probably be somewhat similar, just a little more detailed, and then we start getting to the juicy stuff because now you can't answer with your head anymore. You can only answer with your heart. That's where the true passion lies. That's where your why lies, waiting for you to find it.

So find your why and dig deep and make it personal. If you're crying when you're saying it, it's probably it, and if you're not, it's probably not. Your why is key because it reminds you why you have to get out of bed every day. It reminds you why you have to keep going and keep putting the hours in. It reminds you why it's worth it, the good days, the bad days, the long nights, and the sleepless ones. It's all worth it because it's part of your why and part of your passion, which means it's part of your heart. It's part of you.

Finding this why, now this could take a moment. It could take months. I just worked with one of my buddies by trying to help him discover his "why." It took him months, but he found it. The experience was an awesome moment when he did. I'm proud of him for putting in that work. When you figure it out, now it's time to put it to work. How can you align that why with your life? How can it become one and the same where your why is resembled in what you do on a daily basis? If I have so much passion for it, and I get to live it daily, I'm going to get this great thing called fulfillment. That's better than happiness. Robin Williams said it best, "Happiness is fleeting."

When you wear a shirt that fits perfectly that day, it feels just right. You get a kind of happy feeling when that happens like when you get a new car, a new hat, a new game or a new phone. You might be happy, but when that new wears off, you go back to the same. Happiness is fleeting. It's short term. It's temporary. Fulfillment? You know, like Tony Robbins says, "That's forever." Fulfillment can never be taken away, for it is a forever-type thing. It doesn't go away. It doesn't fade. Fulfillment, that feeling, you hold onto it for a lifetime.

When you align your life with your passion, and you made it

your purpose, which is your why, you are in another state. This state is more smiles and high energy. It's more celebrations. It's more good days than bad. It's more good moments than bad moments. Why? Even the bad ones, even the ones that used to destroy you at your other job that you didn't really care about, when they happen, you know why you're doing it. So it's okay. It's all right. We will take it. It's fine to come our way because it means that much to us.

So you align your life with your why, that becomes your purpose, your calling, and everybody gets to experience the gift of you and the gifts we have. We all have strengths. We already talked about this. I promise no one has no strengths. Well, we're told all too often to look at our weaknesses and try to improve them rather than look at our strengths and double, triple, and quadruple them. Go all in on them. Gary V. says that often, "Go all in on your strengths." He's one of many. I happen to agree with him. Go all in on you and whatever it is that you're really good at and all you care about. I mean it's on your mind all the time because it is part of you. You thinking about it makes your heart leap when you do it, so go for it. Make that your life. Make that your calling. Let everybody experience your gift. Let them all see your masterpiece. Not everyone will love it, but the ones that need it will. That's more than enough.

The next thing I would suggest is to find your mountaintop. What's the biggest point that you can see in this field with this passion, this purpose, this calling, this focus, or whatever you wanna call it? What's the highest you can see? I already told you mine earlier in the book. I'm standing on stage. I'm just behind the curtain. I can hear the crowd going crazy. I peek out. I see the seats full, and the balcony's full with people. I see the UnleashU crew right there behind me, all excited, ready for that moment. I give my inner circle one last dap, and I just go out there and let my art all out. Man, I rock that stage. That day people are moved to do bigger and better things than they thought possible. They are ready to show the world their masterpiece.

That's my mountaintop. I haven't gotten there yet. I'm working on it and for it. You have to visualize that mountaintop. You have to see it. You have to feel it. You have to, in every sense you can think of. What would it smell like? What would the air taste like? What would you see? What would you hear? I vision that every day. That's my mountaintop. I envision it every day so I know when I'm there, I'll know because I've been there multiple times in my mind.

So, what's your mountaintop? What's your peak? Here's the great thing, I hope this happens with me, but it can with you as well. I hope that you hit that mountaintop and then see there's a further one, and another one, and another one to keep going for. There is a weird thing that happens to people willing to go for it, when they get there, they form another mountain that they want to climb. They keep creating mountains to destroy. We will find more ways to impact the world with the art we have inside us and with the greatness we all have.

I think of my mom. I think about how she was a nurse, and she was a small business owner while going to school and while raising a family. I think of all the times she thought she hit a peak and then found another one. She even got her Ph.D and a second one. Then discovered she wanted to do Eagala at almost 70. There's always another peak. You'll have more peaks too, but you have to figure out the first one. So what's your first one?

So now that you know where you are and know your mountaintop, now you can make a path. That path doesn't have to be one that's already paved out for you. It doesn't have to be something common that people accept. It has to be the best one for you. What's your passion? What are the steps you can take? Yeah, plan out steps so you can check them off the list when you do them. I have so many lists on little pads, on these little packets of paper with things written all over them.

I have one right now that I'm using to do this book. They're steps because then I can see I'm accomplishing things on the way to the top, and I'm getting closer. Every single line crossed out is a step up the mountain. Yeah, sometimes I have to redirect. Sometimes I have to change ways. You're going to too. That's part of it, and that's okay.

It keeps you on your toes. It keeps you seeing that you have options to get there. You learn from the missteps, but you need to have steps, like little stepping stones. Yes, celebrate them when you achieve them. I'm not saying go out and get roaring drunk or anything but celebrate them. When you achieve them, celebrate. Celebrate small victories. They add up, and its a reminder of the journey. The journey is the best part so enjoy it!

Now that you have some of these steps planned out, conquer one. It's funny, people say the hardest one is the first one. That's normally the case. The hardest part is getting started. It doesn't say it takes all the challenge away, but it makes it easier. Listen, start going to the gym. Go the first day, and on the second day, it'll get easier. Sure, you'll be sore. Sure, you'll probably try to talk yourself out of it. You already did it, and you know you did, and after you accomplish something, of course, you know you can do it again, and again, and again. Like I said earlier as well, when someone else accomplishes something, you know you can because if anyone can, everyone can.

After you take the first step, if you say, "What do you do now? Keep going. I remember when I was younger, I had this basketball coach. He was pretty funny. He used to say all these crazy one-liners, and when I was younger, I had no idea what any of them meant. You know, like how he would be all over you like "white on rice?" I was like, "What? I don't get it." Then, when I became old enough to be able to be a little smart aleck about it, I would say, "What if it's fried rice?"

He once said this phrase, and I think he stole it from Winston Churchill. You know, "If you are in hell, keep going." Well, he used to say, "It's not the fall that kills you, son. It's the sudden stop." I always remember that with everything I do. The fall doesn't kill you, but the stop does. So keep going. Don't stop now. Don't ever stop. Let's say you accomplish your wildest dreams. You are on your mountaintop. Look for another one. We can throw out a million names that probably accomplished their first mountaintop: Bill Gates, Steve Jobs, I mean the list goes on and on. We could throw them all out:

Zuckerberg, etc! I never say his name right. I don't know why. I just call him Mr. Facebook.

Then what did they do when they got to their mountain top? They saw another one. They saw another peak. They went from computers to phones to iPods and iPads, right? You keep expanding. You see something bigger. You see something different. It's like when you're a baby, you're just trying to sit up, and then you're trying to crawl, then you're trying to walk, and then you're trying to run. It's just like that when you're chasing your goals and dreams. It's just like that when you're trying to find your calling. It's a process. Keep going. Don't stop because it's not the fall that kills you, it's the sudden stop.

When I was thinking about who I wanted to use in this chapter as someone that would best resemble your calling, there were so many names and so many great stories that I read. A lot of people in the UnleashU crew were throwing me a bunch of names and different ideas, and I loved them all. They all made sense, but I just kept coming back to this one. There are so many people that quit their jobs and went out in another field. There are so many people that stopped their big corporate job and went and did their thing. There are people that dropped out of school and went and did their thing. We heard of many of them, but there is one that kept sticking out to me that is rarely used and is the best in this situation: Theodore Geisel.

You might not know him by that name because in 1927 he changed his name to Dr. Seuss. What I didn't know was that during his stint in college where he planned on getting an English literature degree, actually, a Ph.D. in it, as Dr. Seuss, he gave it up; he quit school on behalf of his college sweetheart. She was telling him to go follow drawing. Well, in 1928, they got married. Less than 10 years later, he wrote his first manuscript. You know, his first one was rejected almost 30 times? Almost 30 times, it was rejected and flat out denied. This man had to leave school and quit the idea that he thought he had to do in order to make it. He left to follow his drawing interests and wrote a manuscript after working in advertisement for multiple companies throughout that time, and then he gets rejected almost 30 times.

What's funny is the person that accepted it is famous for saying this quote, he said, "I had a lot of great writers, but there was only one genius on my author list, and that was Dr. Seuss." Unfortunately, he passed away in 1991. By that time, he sold over 600 million copies of his book in over 20 languages. If that's not a famous failure, it's not just someone that knew his calling no matter what he had to go through that was just willing to battle it. You don't think his passion carried him through? You don't think that knowing this was his calling, and that he was supposed to do this, proved he was meant to share his gift?

Theodore Geisel / Dr. Seuss

He could have quit numerous times. He could have went back to his roots. He had some ground to fall back on and he always could of went back to school. You don't think he would have if he just didn't know? He didn't put in those times, those days, when no one knew who he was when he sold zero copies of any book without knowing. When he was getting rejected on the first script he wrote, you think if he didn't know this was meant for him that he wouldn't be able to keep going?

When you know something's made for you and you know you're meant for it, no matter what the rejection is, no matter what the hardship is, and no matter how many people tell you you can't, you'll keep going because it's your purpose. It's your calling. It's your passion. It makes you fight for it, and makes you learn and grow for it. The only way we can get as far as we can is if we have that thing inside us that won't let us stop when everyone says we should, that won't let us quit when it gets too hard, and when the amount of scars we tally up means nothing from the pounding of our heart.

Even with all that rejection and all that doubt, you still know. Listen, some days I wake up, and I go, "Man, maybe this isn't meant for me. Maybe I'm not good enough for this. Maybe I don't reach enough people. Maybe I can't help. Maybe I'm wasting everyone else's time including my own," and remember, I already said time is the biggest resource and the greatest resource of them all. Maybe that's the case. I take a deep breath, and that voice inside me says, "Stop talking stupid. It's not gonna be easy because you wanna do something extraordinary. It's gonna be hard, but you were made for this hard. So whatever comes with it, you were built for it."

Now, know this, you are built for whatever you want, whatever your wildest dream is, whatever your biggest passion is, whatever keeps you going, and whatever excites you beyond the rest. You were built for it. Not just the finished product of it, but you were built for the rough days, the bad days, and the sad days. You were built for the times where you think about quitting. Just don't. You were built for all those times. You were built for this very moment to get to the moment that you consider your mountaintop. You were made for it. It's your gift, and you're supposed to share it with all of us. So get to it, but remember, you were made for it.

So what's your purpose? What's your why? How can you align it with your life? See your mountaintop, plan the steps, take the first one, and don't stop. Dr. Seuss the shit out of your life. I look forward to hearing about it. Now, what are you waiting for?

Chapter 6

EASY NOW, TIGER!
MY GRANDMOTHER SAID, "PAZENZA."

"Our patience will achieve more than out force." – Edmund Burke

Easy, one step at a time. What I mean by that is that key phrase you probably hear from lots of people: it's called patience or as my family used to say, "pazenza." I think it's time for patience. You're going to need it. This life is a marathon not a sprint. Reaching the mountain tops we talked about last chapter is not a fast thing. I love speed, but you need it for the long haul.

I used to hate when I was younger, even now sometimes I still hate it. I want something so bad, and I'm working towards it. I'm eager for it, and I'm putting myself in position to get it. I want it, and I want it now. I always equate it to new shoes or the new coat that I want. I don't care if it's summer; if it's a coat I really want, I have to get that coat. It's 100 degrees out, and I still need a coat. It doesn't make sense, right? Neither does this. Full disclosure–I have bought a coat when it was extremely hot out, but it doesn't make it right. It wasn't even on sale! Crazy, I know.

It's tough to do something amazing. It's tough to live your best life. It's not easy to get to because if it was, we'd all be doing it right now, and this book would be pointless or at least this chapter of the book. So if it was easy to look like a shredded calendar guy or girl, we'd all do it, but it's not easy: it's hard and takes countless time, takes extreme amount of effort, and takes soul wrenching dedication. It takes getting up over and over again when you get knocked down. Getting through all the struggle, the loss, the sacrifice, and all the stuff that we don't want to talk about, that we know is part of it, actually a big part of it.

There's a reason why I said, "Look at a mountaintop," and then right after I said, "What's the first step?" And I know at this point in the book you're probably thinking, "Wow," trying to remember all these different things and trying to memorize all these different steps, "I really want this best life he's talking about. I want the best life. I'm gonna get it now, I want it now." The problem is you can't get it now, but you can take the steps to get it. I'll tell you this too, you might not be able to get it now, but you can lose it now: by not doing the necessary steps, by not keeping your eye on the prize, by not staying focused, and by not doing all the things we spoke about in the last chapters.

This is probably the hardest chapter for me to do. This isn't the hardest chapter for me to talk about or to get through, but this is one of the hardest ones for me to actually do. It's the patient part, but I have to remember there's a process. Nolan Ryan didn't start out by striking out every major-leaguer. He worked his way up. Michael Jordan didn't start out by knocking down game winning shots to win NBA titles. He started by getting cut from his high school varsity team and playing J.V. There's a process, and for everyone it's different, but there is a process for everyone.

I get this argument all the time with people around me because they'll use a phrase like, "God-given ability' or 'just natural talent," and I feel like we use those things to make it easier for us to acknowledge the fact that the person worked that hard to be that good at the craft, or that they honed their skills to be one of the best that ever did it, or that great at it, or to achieve greatness in it. There's a process. I say step one, so clearly we should know there's going to be a step two after we do step one, and so on and so on, 'til you get to your mountaintop, 'til you reach your goal.

I love this phrase that Jocko Willink says. Check him out if you like anything like this. He's amazing at his crafts. He says, "Rome wasn't built in a day, but it wasn't destroyed in one either." What you're doing today is going to impact you five years from now, either positively or negatively. Listen, if you have a good diet, if you're working out, if you're drinking plenty of water, in five years from now you will thank you. Now, if you're like me a little bit, you enjoy a soda here and there, have an adult beverage here or there, eat not the best foods here and there, your five-year self isn't thanking you as much. It's probably cursing you a little bit, because there's a process, and you are messing with it.

Listen, if you go to the gym today, you're not going to have ripped abs tomorrow. No, but if you start today, you have a chance of having them down the road if you continue the process. That's life. Life is a process. Listen, we start out by not being able to hold our own heads up, completely dependent on everybody around us. I mean, you throw me in the middle of the pool when I'm a baby, and it's over if someone does not jump in to save me. I have to hope that someone in the area is nice enough to get their nice outfit wet. If you throw me in the pool now, I'm swimming out of it because the process happened.

I couldn't hold my head up, but then I did. I couldn't sit up, but then I did. I couldn't crawl, but then I did. I couldn't walk, but then I did. I couldn't run, but then I did. I didn't know how to speak, but then I did. The process happened. I am beating this over the top because I have to make sure you are getting it. It wasn't overnight, and it wasn't the next day. It wasn't immediately just because I decided it's what I wanted to do. "Today I want to be an author." No, the process takes time. Writing this book takes time. The first book took a lot of time, and there wasn't as much research as this one was. It wasn't that in depth as this one is. You can tell by the word count and probably the page count, but it was still a process. That process does this unfortunate thing called, take time. George Harrison told us all about precious time in his hit song "Got my Mind Set on You". He wasn't kidding you because it takes a whole lot of precious time.

It takes time, and sometimes it takes a lot of time, so much time that they say it takes 10,000 hours of practice to master a subject, skill, trait, or craft. 10,000 hours. Think about it like this, if you work two hours every day on this, two hours every day just on practicing your craft, not doing paperwork, not texting, not scrolling through Facebook, like actually practicing your craft, 10,000 hours, two hours a day, you did not reach mastery level in that year. Not in a year, you're not even close. What, are you roughly over 730 hours? 730 hours if you do two hours a day? Listen, I promise you you're not going to do two hours a day.

There's a shooting instructor, his name's Dave Hopla, love him. He used to work at camps, and then I would bring him in with the teams I coached because he was a great presenter and speaker. He'd always say, "Who shoots hoops every day? Raise your hand." You know every kid's trying to raise their hand now trying to say they do. It's the thing you do.

He's like, "All right, you shot hoops on June 31st?" And the kid would be, "Yes, I did." He would follow up with, "That's not a day." What I'm saying is, and what he was saying is, that you don't do it every day. That was his job, and he didn't do it every day. Nobody shoots hoops every day. I would bet that LeBron doesn't shoot hoops every day. There are rest days, there is vacation with family and friends, and there are different things that happen. Life happens some days when you just can't do it, but know that, if it's true that it takes 10,000 hours to master a craft, start putting them in because it's gonna take time. A whole lot of it. It's not gonna be fun the whole time. We know that already.

There's this great story. It's passed down through generations of this man who had this creaky board. We all know that one in your house that you just step on, it's like creeeeeeaaaaaak, and it drives you crazy every time. That creak in the board makes that horrible sound and makes you cringe. Well, he had one of those boards, and he wanted it fixed because he was having a big event the whole town was coming over for. He was calling every carpenter he could to come, and no one can fix the board. There was one carpenter left, and he was known as the master carpenter. He was trying to avoid him because he cost more money. He didn't want to spend the money, but at this point, he felt like he had no choice. So he called this master carpenter over.

The master carpenter walked around, walked around some more, stepped on the floor, kept walking around, stepping on the floor some more, listening. Finally, after ten minutes of walking around he just stopped, took one nail out and a hammer and hammered into the floor. He looked at the guy and said, "The board's done. No more creaking. That horrible sound is gone, and here's your bill."

The bill was for $100 dollars, and the owner of the house was so distraught and was so upset. He said, "$100 dollars? It took you ten minutes just to do that. $100 dollars?" He's like, "Tell me, how do you justify this?" And the guy took the bill back, and he wrote, $2 dollars for the nail and $98 dollars to know where to hammer it." It's all about mastering your craft. He was the only one that knew where to put it, so he could charge what he wanted. He was the master carpenter in that area, and the value he added was worth the money because he put in the time.

Do you feel like you've mastered anything? Are you on your way to master something? Any craft of yours, any talent of yours, a passion of yours, your purpose or calling, have you mastered it? Have you dedicated yourself enough to it to have the 10,000 hours or more needed to feel it? Have you put in the work and the time? Have you gone through the grind to get it? I'm asking you these questions not to be rude or mean, and I don't know if you have or haven't, that's for you to answer honestly with yourself. I'm asking you because I want you to know how hard it is. I want you to be able to be honest with yourself and say, "I have to put this in to be able to get this out. I've been coasting. I haven't even mastered my own calling." If you haven't mastered your calling, what have you mastered? Always remember you will have to put it in to be able to get it out.

That's why I always give parents a break. When I work with people that are parents and they talk about wanting to be a good dad or mom, I always say, "Listen, being a parent is something we learn as we go and master as we take on." You ever notice the firstborn? Oh, everything's so nerve wracking. They bump their knee, "Oh no! Is everything okay? Do we have to take him to the doctor? Let's go to the ER." The second or third kid, they fall and bump their knee, "Get up, you're fine."

Why is that? We've gotten more comfortable in the craft of parenting. We understand it better. We know it better. We can perform it better. Now, I'm not saying ignore your kid and tell him he's fine. I'm saying we understand that they are not this fragile, little creature that we think they are in the beginning. Why? We don't know any better and because we haven't mastered it. We haven't had the hours, dedication, and time to do it, because becoming a parent, now that's hard to practice for. That's hard to prepare for: you can prepare financially, you can prepare your house, you can prepare the environment and the culture, and all that good stuff, but being a parent, you're learning as you go. Now thank whoever it is you want to thank because your craft doesn't have to be that way. Your craft you can practice. You can perfect your craft. You have to put the time in. You have to earn your stripes.

I remember being young. I was a teenager, and I was trying to find a job. I went to this corner store, and they had a little sandwich shop with a little restaurant. They didn't have many tables or chairs, just a little one, and just a couple people, but at my age it was fine. I went in and said, "I wanna be your manager." I had no idea what I was talking about. The guy was hilarious, now. At the time, I didn't even know what he was talking about.

He said, "Okay, you wanna be the manager? Not a problem. What do you know how to do?"

I didn't know what managers did, so I said, "I know how to manage." Now I'm a teenager remember this.

He goes, "Oh, perfect. Did you manage before?"

"Ah, sold some baseball cards and candies to people in the community."

"Well, that's good," he said. "I got a job for you. Come back tomorrow, start working." So I went back the next day, it was 4:00 after school. He gave me an apron, and he gave me a tub and said, "Collect the dishes and start cleaning them." So now I do this, but I think I'm the manager, I don't know managers don't do this. Even though I think managers should do it, but that's a different topic and a different story for a different book.

So I'm back there cleaning them, and the cook comes over and is like, "Hey, you're the new guy?"

I go, "Yeah, I'm the manager."

That guy's face, I'll never forget how hard he laughed at me. He said, "Just so you're aware, the manager's spot you have is called busboy."

I was taken back, and was like, "Man, that hurt. I thought I was the manager." I went to the guy that gave me the interview, who ends up being the owner and manager, and I said, "I thought I was the manager. You hired me as a manager."

"Right, but you can't start at that. You have to earn your stripes. You have to show everybody that you're manager material."

I didn't even understood what he meant then, but I went home and asked my mom and dad, "What does earning your stripes mean?" My dad loved the question. It was all about earning the opportunity. How many times do we say we deserve an opportunity rather than we earned this opportunity? It's paramount for us in the calling of our life to earn the stripes, to earn the opportunities, to perfect the craft, and to be able to give back to it, not only the craft, but the people around it and the people involved, the people in your community and the people all over the world.

I have this band on; it's in honor of my brother. We have a nonprofit in his name. On it it says, "Be the change." On my business card it says, "Be the change." On the sign in front of our office it says, "Be the change." Everybody says, "Yeah, I wanna do that," and I say, "Awesome, what do you want to change? Do you want to change your family? Do you want to change yourself? Do you want to change your community? Do you want to change the world? What do you want to change? In order to change it, you have to be prepared, and you have to be able to execute. You have to perfect your craft. You need to keep pounding on that sword until it's ready to fight with, until you can defend yourself and everyone else with it."

All this starts with one step. One step, one achievement. Next step, next achievement. Next step, next achievement. In between that next step, next achievement is going to be a fail, failure, rejection, self-doubt, hard work, sacrifice, struggle, and sleepless nights. There's a bunch of little things in between that one that you have to get through, that you have to fight through. It's not going to be easy. It's going be tiresome. There are going be days you don't wanna do it.

There are going to be days you complain, you're sick and tired, and you want stay in bed. There are going to be days that you'd rather do anything else. There will be days that you'd rather play video games, you'd rather go watch sports with your friends or watch the games with your friends, or you'd rather go sit in the bar and have a drink. I'm not saying you have to do this, or that you can't do any of those. I'm not saying all day every day just be perfecting your craft. You can if you want. I'm fine with the two. It's your choice, but know if you're not, if you are giving it no time, you'll never get there.

The other part of this is your calling, your goal, your desire, your mountaintop, is someone else's too. You're not the only one that wants to be the best at writing, or the best lawyer, or the best coach, or the best counselor, or the best therapist, or the best basketball player, or the best football player, or any of the things you can name that you want to be. The best author, the best speaker, whatever it is, someone else wants it too. That's their mountaintop because they're fighting for it. They're willing to dedicate themselves. Like Les Brown says, "You're going day and night for it." They're willing to go and put in the steps. They're willing to work. They are willing to earn the stripes. They're willing to take the time. They are willing to trust the process and go through it. They're willing to spend over 10,000 hours to master a craft. 10,000 hours, think about how many hours that is.

Remember earlier in the book, I talked about you have 100 hours a week that's not spent on necessities, eating, bathroom, or sleeping? 100 hours. To think you need 10,000 or more to master a craft and all you have is 100 hours a week, how are you spending those hours? How precious are those hours, and what are you spending them on? What are you doing with them? Then if you're not … if you don't have enough, how can you get enough? Are you willing to sacrifice some sleep for it? Are you willing to sacrifice less Netflix time for it? Are you willing to sacrifice watching some of the games for it? Less bar time for it? What are you willing to sacrifice to get to where you want to get to? What are you willing to put in? What are you willing to give up to get it?

This is tough. This isn't easy. This is hard stuff. I never told you it would be easy, I told you it would be worth it, and it will be. If you don't believe me, ask Jim Carrey. Jim Carrey you know as an actor, a comedian, even an entrepreneur, and a really big giver in those communities and people's lives. It wasn't always like that. His early age and early career were filled with failure and also scarcity because they really didn't have much except for poverty.

When Jim Carrey was 15 years old, when he was a teenager, his family ran into horrible financial problems. They had to move. At one point it was so bad that they had to live in a van, one of those Volkswagen vans that are coming back into style. They had to move into a van until they could get money back to get back into a house. It was so bad that as a teenager he had to work in a wheel factory, and he had to be a janitor after school for 8 hour shifts or more. Now, there's nothing wrong with being a janitor; it's an honest profession. I always loved that conversation that President John Kennedy had at NASA when he asked the janitor what he does here, and he says, "I help spaceships fly. I'm going to land on the moon," something like that. He had to do these things for his family to be able to make it. I remember at one point, Jim Carrey says a story about how he wrote a $10 million dollar check and put it in his wallet until he could cash it. He said he had 10 years to cash it and then within that 10 year period, he could.

It wasn't the only hardship for Jim Carrey. His first time doing a stand-up gig in his hometown, in the Toronto area, he was literally booed offstage. He bombed it and was heckled, laughed at, pointed at, and made fun of. It was almost like a Jerry Seinfeld experience, the same thing happened to Jerry, but he kept at it. Jim Carrey actually dropped out of high school to go after his passion, knowing that he had to put in the time to be able to get it. When he dropped out at 17 years old, he found his way to California. He actually landed a stand-up gig in Hollywood. During this time, he married what he thought was his sweetheart and thought he was on his way, but five years later his marriage failed. The stand-up gig turned into nothing, but he kept at it not accepting failure as his destination, and then went into acting.

It took 11 years for him just to get an opportunity to appear on a real, TV show that was known, and you might know it as In Living Color. It took him 11 years just to appear on it. That was his break, and that was his opportunity. You know what? It took 4 more years after that for him to get his biggest break of all, and that was to star in Ace Ventura: Pet Detective, and the rest is history. 15 years after he moved to Hollywood, he finally got that break. 15 years perfecting his craft, mastering it, not quitting, not giving up, not tucking his head and running, because he knew, like Jocko Willink said, "Rome wasn't built in a day and it wasn't destroyed in one either," that he had to keep going. That it would take time, that he needed to take those 10,000 hours, that it was a process, and that he needed patience. One step at a time.

I know the life you see, the you you wanna be, the best life, the best you, I know how bad you want it, but I also know what you're willing to do to get it. So you don't need it now. Keep giving that time and keep going through the process, trust yourself, and trust the feeling. Know it's worth it and keep going. Earn your stripes. Put in 10,000 plus hours, and if you do that, and you don't stop, you don't quit, you don't say, "Poor me," you don't lay down on that cold, cold ground where so many dreams have died. Just keep going, knowing that it's just part of the process, and it's just part of the steps you have to go through to get to where you want to get to. Jim Carey did, and we all know if anyone can, everyone can.

See that vision, know how grand it is, and have patience because that's how great it's going to be. Greatness, the best, takes time, even if we're talking about the best you living the best life that you can live, by tapping into that greatness within, unleashing yourself in the world, and changing it for the better. By leaving that impact, you'll never die twice. Pazenza, as they told me, pazenza.

Chapter 7

EMBRACE THE SUCK

"*Embrace the suck, for the suck is part of the process.*" – *AJ Jacobs*
"*Don't let the process punk you out of the promise.*" – *Michael Fabber*

There will be a struggle. I promise you. This is probably the toughest chapter I ever wrote. I have to be honest: this was extremely hard. In this chapter, you're going to hear things about my life in depth that I probably never talked to anyone about any of it or at least don't want to remember doing it. I want to show you how real it is and how we all can make it through it. I can't show you that if I do not let you see into my life. I do not want sympathy but an understanding that we will all have many different types of suck and setbacks. The suck will kick our ass and screaming mercy will not stop it. The only solace I can offer is when it takes a break kicking you, get up and push through to another level. Use the suck for you every chance you get. This part of your journey will build the thickest skin, the most I can get through it mentality.

I talked about it a little bit already in every chapter because it's that important, but it wouldn't be as real if I didn't make a chapter for itself. This is the hard stuff. This is the stuff that knocks you on your back and keeps you there. This is the stuff that makes you not want to try or to give in and quit. Don't even get started. This is where our fears lie, but we have to embrace the suck because it comes no matter what. There is no running or hiding from it. Just prepare, take it in, and grow. In my first book I talked about us all taking L's, we will all experience losses in different forms: the lesson losses and the life losses.

First, we'll talk about some obvious ones. Some of the ones I mentioned, we went over in the previous chapters, and we will in the following chapters because it's all part of the journey. It's a constant part of the journey. I wish I could tell you that it isn't only here and there you'll feel it. Along the whole journey, the whole time it will be with you. It is part of you.

I used to fight it so hard. I used to be convinced that I could fight the struggle and anything that life threw at me. I learned later it does not have to be that way, and it cannot be that way. You can't fight the pain but the opposite is actually the best practice. You don't have to go through this stuff alone and angry. You don't have to experience this in a way that is harmful to yourself and your future, but you do have to go through it. As I got older, as I got more honest, as I got more open and got through more trials and tribulations in my life, I don't try to fight it anymore. I do not hide from it or bury it deep inside me anymore. I embrace it because as cliche as it might sound, as after school special as it might seem, the things that have been the hardest have made me the best. I don't mean best as in against anyone else. It's not a sort of ranking. I mean, those are the things that made me better now. Those are the things that made me as good as I could be and will be. Those are the things that made me follow my passions, make it my purpose, and my calling. Be willing to answer that call like the last chapter. These losses showed me what was and who was important to me and how to regularly prioritize my life.

These are the things that even though they knocked me down and sometimes kept me down for a while, made me stronger, braver, and wiser. As hard as that is to believe and as hard as it was to go through, it's true. I think about all of them. Some are super hard. Some made the journey better, but they all left an imprint on my soul. Let's start with the hard stuff. In this struggle, what we have to embrace is the idea of failure. How many great people who you hear about have failed first? Their first companies failed, they failed the first time they tried to invent something, or they failed the first time they tried to get the job of their dreams, their calling, or their passion. How many times do you hear people failing in school, dropping out or getting kicked out? How many times do we hear about people failing in business, getting fired, getting demoted, or not even getting hired? How many times have you heard this? How many times have we went through it ourselves? The failure is part of it. If you have not, it's because you don't want to admit it or are ignoring it for your own reasons, or you never took the chance to really go for something bigger than yourself.

Before we go further I will tell you this, no person is a failure. Failing is an act: it is not a person. A person cannot be a failure, but a person could have failed. I believe that 100%. There is not a single person that is a failure. Every single one of us that has done anything meaningful has failed but are not a failure.

I'm sitting here on my second book. I've had businesses that didn't make it. I've worked jobs that I've gotten fired from or let go from. I've had failed relationships. I've been knocked straight on my ass. I have tried to create things that did not work and be part of things that did not happen. I have failed. I love that one Michael Jordan commercial where he is like, "I have lost this many games in my career, I have missed this many game winning shots. I have missed this many shots. I've had this many turnovers." He lists all the negative things, all the times he failed, and all the times he made a mistake. The commercial ends with him being Michael Jordan and being the greatest. So again if anyone can, everyone can.

Edison, Einstein, you name them, they've been through it. You name the greats, and they've all been there. They have all seen failure, and they've tasted failure's bitterness. It's not a stranger. It's almost like family, how often they see it. Heck, to me its like a shadow now. The next part of this failure mentality, the next disease that sets in us, is doubt. I am not talking about the doubt from the outside. That's fine and will always be there. You're going to get that, and you're going to fight through that and use that as motivation at times. The dangerous one comes in the form of self-doubt. The self-doubt kills more dreams and ideas than anything else. You know the busiest day of the week is? Some day. Oh, I'll do that someday, or I will get to it someday. I have not seen that day on any calendar, have you? What you're saying is I don't believe in doing it or myself enough to try it now.

There is a bunch of things we say, "I don't have time." Meaning, I'm not committed to make the time. "I'm not good enough." I'm not committed to get better to be good enough to do it. "I don't have the connections." That means, I'm not going to take the time to go meet the people to be able to perform the way that I need to have that job. All that is, is when you say something like that, it's just an excuse to yourself and is the reason why you won't do it. Why you won't do it is because somewhere in your mind, knowing or not knowing, you're telling yourself you can't. Either you're not good enough, smart enough, wealthy enough, creative enough, or talented enough, whatever it is that you're telling yourself, and it's holding you back.

Self-doubt is a killer. I can't talk about self-doubt enough. Self-doubt could break you and could make you never try, and that can make you never try it again. Both of them are horrible. You remember when I said a little while ago that no one can be a failure? When you stop going for your purpose, your passion, or your calling, you aren't a failure, but you are for damn sure failing. You stop fighting for the best you and the best life, maybe then. Maybe when you quit, that's only part of it. So if you haven't given it another chance yet, get back at it. You can always flip the script. Do not accept failure! Learn and go at it again.

I was thought to be a failure multiple times. Remember this is the guy that failed third grade. Failure. Remember this is the guy that used to have to walk down the hallway to the reading classes two grades below the grade he was in. Failure. This is the guy that said to be taken out of school to be taught a trade. Why? I was a failure. This was the guy who was told he would be dead or in jail by 21. Why? I was a failure. I am the guy that failed at multiple businesses. Failure. Throughout all those times, I could have believed them. That self-doubt could have sunk into my mind and believe me at times, it did. Heck, at times it still does.

I opened a restaurant called Jammin Joes in honor of my brother, of course. Let me tell you I bit way more off than I could handle. I was there everyday, all day and still couldn't keep up. I learned so much through failure. but I didn't see it that way at the time. I learned how to bartend, cook, manage, lead, communicate and learned patience. Oh, and I became the man at Mega Touch and Miss Pacman games. It was a Caribbean beach bar and grill, a really cool joint. We had the best burgers, wings, and jerk chicken I have ever tasted still to this day. We hammered away daily for four years to make this place something special and known. A place that people would come into a beach town to go to and enjoy. We had music Thursday through Sunday and all kinds of entertainment. It was chill for sure. For years I would stand outside and sell, sell, sell, to try to get people to give us a chance. Finally, year four was here, and we were making it! We were having the best year of the business to date, and summer was just about to kick off. It was Father's Day, and I had no idea what was coming for me. A waiter and friend named Dan was pouring a glass of milk and asked if I could smell it because it smelled like smoke. We both thought that was odd, so when I looked back to make a joke over his shoulder, all I saw out the back door was fire. I of course, yell "Shit. Fire!" He was still talking about the milk because he wasn't aware of what was growing mere feet behind him. I ran by grabbed the ice bucket that was full of ice and water and threw it on the fire. It seemed to lower it enough to get control of it. I threw the hose into the sink area and said, "Hook it up." I wasn't aware they hooked it up to the old sink that the water was turned off on. So when I tried to use it, I would have had a better chance pissing on it at that point. The fire came back with a vengeance, and when the propane safety feature kicked in, it was over. The place burned down and all was lost. I didn't think we really needed that much fire coverage due to location and a plain lack of understanding. When all was said and done, we lost six figures, and the business, we spent four years on creating, was gone for good!

I'm going to give credit to my mom and dad again because both in their own way, made sure I knew what it took to be successful and made sure I knew I could. That's why I tell you this: anyone can, and everyone can. Unleash your greatness and live your best life. Another tough one is that nasty word: rejection. Like I told you about when I asked that girl out on a date, maybe not a date, I don't even know what I was trying to do, but I damn sure remember that feeling of a hard NO. Rejection is tough whether you're getting rejected from the job you wanted, getting rejected from the relationship you wanted, getting rejection from anything, or getting rejected from the school you want to get in or the apartment or house you want, or the car loan when you think you're going to take that next step. There's never a time where rejection is this fantastic thing. Rejection is a mystical creature. It's not a unicorn.

Yes, sometimes people get rejected, and it was a gift. And sometimes people get rejected, and they just keep fighting till they don't. Sometimes people just accept it. Don't be that one. Do not accept rejection as a permanent answer. It is a short-term obstacle, not a life time stop sign. You know the best way to beat rejection? Hard work, dedication, and being relentless. That's the greatest cure. Hard work, everyone it is that easy but will not be easy. We have a phrase we use at Unleash Unow, and it's O.W.E every day. O-W-E every day. O.W.E. every day. It stands for out work everyone every day. See, you don't control if you're the smartest one in the room. I hope you're not, no offense, that's not a dig. If you're the smartest one in the room, you're not in a big enough room, get to a bigger one now.

If you are the funniest one in the room, you don't control it. If you're the coolest one in the room, you don't control it. If you're the one with the most style in the room, you don't control it. The one with the most connections, you don't control that. The one with the coolest watch, you don't control that. So what you do control is this: your attitude, your effort, and how you treat people. You also control how hard you work (effort). Remember one of my first battle cries, O.W.E., Out Work Everyone!

So, every day put more in and fill the glass higher and give more. I promise you, no matter how skilled you are, no matter how smart you are, no matter what connections you have or don't have, no matter if you're the coolest one, or the one no one talks to, people will notice. Not only will they notice, they'll want you there. They'll want that effort, that desire, that dedication, higher and higher. So, we live by this simple phrase, O.W.E every day, out work everyone.

Yes, that sometimes means long hours. Believing right now it's nighttime, right now is dark, right now is Halloween. It is Halloween night, and I'm doing this. Why? I'm willing to put it in because I know that's the only way I can get it out. The only chance I have to get anything out is by putting it in. You have to give it if you want a chance to receive it. What I want to get out is to reach one. If I don't make this content, if I don't write this book, if I don't tell you my heart to hopefully touch yours, I know I never will. So, you're going to put in those hours. You're going to sacrifice. You already do. Here's my thing. This is what I tell people, you're sacrificing family time right now for your job. If you go to work at all. If you go and do work, you're sacrificing family time for that. The drive between the house and office and the hours spent per day doing it. You're looking at 8 to 12 hours a day sacrificing your time doing something that you might or might not care about or are passionate about. If you are going to give that time to something and away from other things that you truly care about regardless, wouldn't it be better to be passionate about it? If it's going to happen anyway might as well make it count towards something magical, towards something that makes your heart leap and gives you fulfillment.

So, when I say find your passion and follow it, when I first started getting into coaching, it was turning your passion to your profession. If you're going to spend that amount of time doing something, make it something that you love and make it something that makes your heart leap and something you couldn't imagine not doing. Make it something that you fight for, that you would crawl for, that you would scrape yourself up to the bone for, you would bleed for, you would be tired for, and you would miss sleep for. I'm not going to sleep to do this. I love it.

If you're going to give that time, if you're going to sacrifice these things, at least sacrifice it for something that means so much. Now, all that is part of the struggle. All that is part of embracing the suck, but we haven't hit the meat yet. We've only seen the tip of the iceberg. This is the hardest part: loss, the life kind. This is this part that's still brings tears to my eyes years later. This is the part that I have learned that I can't explain. This is the part that doesn't sit right with me, but this is part of it and a big part. The losses I've taken changed my life. It could have changed it for the worst. I don't know how I got lucky, but I know the amount of loss now I've had could have left me flat on the mat. I had to change the way I looked at it because I don't think I would make it if I didn't.

When I was 12 years old, my brother, Joey, took his own life. If you read my first book, *Your Story: You Have Every Reason to Quit, but Don't.* You remember this time I said, that I woke up seeing my mom hit the floor crying. I said I had two choices: close my eyes and stay in the dream, or open them and walk towards my nightmare. I can't tell you about what I had for breakfast yesterday. I don't remember, but I can tell you everything about that day. It's still so vivid. My sister standing there crying. My mom on the floor crying and my dad standing there trying to figure out what to do. My dad was a mountain of a man. The toughest man I ever even heard about, books wouldn't do this kind of toughness justice.

This might have been the one and only time I saw him cry. I saw him lost. It wasn't a weeping, tears running down, sobbing type of cry. It is just the irritated eyes, one teardrop just crest on the side of his nose. I knew how bad that moment was going to be. My brother died a couple of days before his 20th birthday. He took his own life. He was a smart man, and he was a good-looking, young man. He was in the National Guard and in the service. He had his whole future in front of him, his whole life, and then, he was gone. He was going to be something special, and we all knew it. He was the chosen one, of the 4 boys, he had the whole package. But sometimes we get to a place where we cannot see how amazing it will all be. I didn't know how to handle that, and I still don't really.

The community was amazing. I don't think we had to make food for a week or two. People were so nice. I was young, I really didn't know what I was supposed to do or how to act. So, I did this crazy thing, I didn't. I didn't handle it. I just tucked it down deep inside of me. I just kept playing basketball. Later in middle school an upperclassmen who was a basketball player I looked up to passed away due to cancer. I stuffed that away. In high school, a buddy of mine, Matt Allen, passed away in a car accident. I literally saw him less than an hour before it happened. I stayed at work because my boss at the time asked me to stay late, or I would of been with him. I stuffed that away. As I keep getting older, I keep getting more angry. I had the "it's not fair attitude," that "me against the world attitude." I remember we talked about that earlier, nothing's fair. I didn't know that at that point. I just said it wasn't, and I believed I was getting a raw deal.

A couple years go by and I'm a teenager, 19. My buddy wakes me up, Anthony Ferris, on another night I'll never forget. He wakes me up panicking. I'm like, "What's up? What is it?" He says, "The hospital called. Your mom and dad are at the hospital. You got to call them. It sounds important, man." I was like, "What?" I call and at this point, I don't even know who it is. I don't know what happened. I'm definitely scared, but I don't want to show it. We all went out that night. So, I didn't have my car because I didn't drive. I just rode with some friends.

So, he woke me up. We didn't have any way to get to the hospital. I remember Ferris going door to door till someone would take us. I never will forget it was Melly, Mel one time, LOL or at least that's what we called him. He got up in the middle of the night and took me and Ferris to the hospital and stayed there the entire night till the next morning. I remember getting to the hospital, and they brought me in, and I saw my mom. She was talking to me. We were sitting there for a while, and they came up to us and they said, "We're going to move you to another room here." They moved us to this little room with four couches, very little ones. At most like you maybe could fit two people on it, maybe. You know that kind where its awkward for two people, it's really for one person, but it's like you can fit two people if you don't mind being on top of one another. It's not that awkward I guess at that moment, but in the clear moment, it sure is.

There are tissues literally on every side of you. I found out that night that room is for when the person you care about is going to die room. They don't want people to see it. They do not want others to see that scene. So, they put you by yourself with a couple of awkward couches and a lot of tissues. I remember the doctor walking in and telling my mom that my father had passed away. I remember the shock. I never thought that man would die. Honestly, sometimes I think he was still alive. Especially after I remember coming to my mom's house one night very late, and I saw his truck, and this stunned me. It was like, "Oh no, he's going to get me." He was already passed away for a little while, but his impact was still felt and is still felt.

This is when I learned that my mom was stronger than anyone I knew, the strongest person period. The doctor told her that, and the first thing she said to me was, "How am I going to tell your sister?"

I said, "Don't worry about that right now." My sister was on a cruise at the time. She had a couple days left on her vacation. My mom's initial thought wasn't she lost the love of her life, her best friend for 20, 30 years, it was what am I going to tell your sister? That selfless love is something I aspire to have for people. It stills boggles my mind to have that care for others when your world is crumbling around you.

So, my dad was gone. It was sudden; he wasn't sick. It just happened. I got even more angry, but now it's hard to keep it down. I got into fights. I had a couple of run-ins with the law. Chucky, the brother of my buddy Anthony Ferris, passed away a couple of months later. They were the kind of guys you love to have on your side but hated to be against. They were annoying and scrappy but loyal and dedicated. They were the friends you'd love to have, and the enemy you hated to have. I hated seeing him that way. We went out the night of his brother's funeral, and I'll never forget it. There was this tire ... So, the tire popped off the truck. The tire is running down the white line on the side of the road, and I just could see something on the side of the road. So, I'm staring at that side of the road trying to figure out what the heck is running at us. I thought it was a bear or a dog or some sort of animal, trying to figure out what it's going to do, but the whole time I'm missing the sparking, flaming truck that is on fire coming straight at us.

I see Ferris like putting his legs on the dashboard, and of course, I wonder, "What he is doing?"

This truck goes by. I just noticed that when it goes by my window he goes, "Wow, man. I want to live."

I said, "I noticed the tire on the way, and I missed the flames coming out of his truck next to me." It's funny how sometimes what we focus on. I just kept bottling this stuff in trying to prove I was tough and trying to prove I couldn't be affected by life. Years and years go by. In 2011, all that changed. A man I asked to be in my wedding party, I looked at as one of my best friends, took his own life. Man, he was an amazing man. I envied him. He was great. He was there when you needed him and always willing to give a helping hand. He played games well and played all kinds of sports with you. He was a great athlete. He was a great dad. It seemed like he was great at everything. We had Coronas and watched Celtics games together. We talked hoops and life at a level many do not feel comfortable doing, especially at 30 years old.

He used to always come up to the school I was coaching at and play at open gyms with us. He would teach the players different moves and life lessons. We used to rent these gyms out sometimes and just play ball in them. We played pickup, flag football for years and always matched up against one another. I remember one New Year's Eve he was at my house, we were having a little New Year's eve gathering and my daughter was there. She was young, maybe 4 years old. Man, he was just playing with her so naturally like they had this great relationship. He just kept playing with her. He was playing with her so much that I literally had to say like, "Listen, you don't have to play with her. You're being really cool and nice but you don't have to do it." It felt like it was some burden. He looked at me smiled and made sure I knew he was having a ball doing it. We had some great laughs. Times that I'll forever hang onto.

One afternoon I get a call from him. I was in the yard hitting those fake plastic golf balls. I had to practice to be the next great golfer (I suck at golf). He sounds a little upset on the phone but nothing that would drive me to the point to think anything was up. That could be because I WAS TOO BUSY HITTING PLASTIC GOLF BALLS!!! I wasn't all in on the conversation. I wasn't giving him what he deserved or what he needed. He said he was going through some things, and I asked if he wanted to hangout. He passed. He wanted to be alone. I did that cool guy thing where you pass life advice that doesn't help at all like, "It will all be okay, man." Well it wouldn't all be okay ever again.

The day before, they found his body. I drove around everywhere I could go, anywhere I could think of: batting cages, the beach, any ballpark we played at. I drove up to the open gym that night to see if he showed up. I called everybody I could think of that we knew from out of town to ask if he was there. I searched for hours, but I couldn't find him. No one even knew I was doing it except for his family. The next day, I went to work. I got some kind of announcement on the speaker to come to the office where the state trooper was waiting to tell me that he found his body, and he was no longer with us. I couldn't hold this stuff down anymore. I even tried then. I tried the old fashioned way, to just grin your teeth and bear it. I tried with the assistance of adult beverages and other ways to try to keep it down, but it couldn't work. That was it. I couldn't fight it anymore. Now, I knew I was beat, and life got me. I questioned if I was built for this and if I was even worthy enough to have a spot on this earth.

That responsibility feel, that guilt, I'm still here, and they aren't. That I wasn't enough as a friend, that I couldn't save him. I wasn't a good enough brother, I wasn't a good enough son, and I wasn't a good enough person. It was tough. Those were some of the hardest days. This lasted almost a year. I said I would stop fighting. I would just accept what was and accept what happened. I couldn't do anything about it; I couldn't change what already happened. I was worse than a failure, I was the worst.

I tried to be him. I tried to make it like he wasn't gone. I tried to play both myself and him. I tried to play myself and my dad. I tried to play myself and my brother. I tried to play all the ones I lost and myself. I think it was me trying to make the others that loved him not have to go through what I was going through. Maybe it was selfish. Maybe it wasn't. I can't tell you either way. I can tell you trying that was the worst and best thing I ever did. I finally admitted I was broken.

That was when I finally was willing to accept my calling because I wanted to help people. I wanted to be there for people. I wanted them to know they're not alone. I wanted to fight for people. I wear a medallion around my neck, St. Jude. Great Saint of lost causes. He won't quit on you, so you don't quit on you. We're all here for a reason. We all have greatness, and we're meant to share that with the world. All too often we lose people before their time. In America alone, 125 people commit suicide a day. In the world, it's over 3000. It's roughly one every 40 seconds. Till that number is zero, I did not do my job.

So many people with so many gifts to give us, so many people with so many talents that we can see, so many people with that greatness still there waiting to be tapped, and we never get them. Until that number is zero, I have a job to do. Last year, I lost two more of my good friends. I lost my man, Wig. I lost one of my best friends when I was younger, Anthony Ferris. Lost both to overdoses, way before their time. It wasn't like it was before with me, with loss.

I celebrated the life they had. I celebrated the great times we had. I celebrated the lessons I learned from them. I celebrated all the laughs, all the times I'll never forget, all the times that I knew someone was there for me because of them and that I'll get to be that for someone else. I don't suffer the loss now, I celebrate the time. I know that sounds corny, but I do. I thank God every day I had these people in my life that cared about me that guided me. That taught me lessons in life and in death because the loss is part of it. It's part of the journey; that's the toughest part of it. Definitely the toughest part but it's part of it and a big part.

I don't tell you my story to feel bad for me. I don't tell you these things of loss because I want your sympathy. I tell them to you because I want you to know I've been there where you've been because we've all experienced this loss. Some loss is harder to get over, but like everything else, it's all how you look at it. Was it fair that I lost so many people way before their time? You could say, no, but what's fair? What is that? I don't look at it like that. I look at it as I'm thankful. I'm thankful that I had the opportunity to have those people in my life to give me those gifts and to let me experience that love and hopefully, give love to them.

One of my favorite people in history is Abraham Lincoln. You can read a book a million times over about Abraham Lincoln for how amazing he was as a person. Was he perfect? No. None of us are. I'm not saying that. He was an amazing person, all that he suffered and went through but kept going. How many times did he have to embrace the suck, and how many times did he have to struggle in so many different ways from loss to mental health illness, to willing to stand and die for what he believed in?

Abraham Lincoln

Abraham Lincoln was the 16th president, in case you didn't know. Remember abolishing slavery, right? He wanted to free slaves in America, and he wanted equal rights way before the time where people thought that was really something. No one talks about what Abraham Lincoln had to go through. That at 23 years old he found himself jobless because he got fired. He also lost a bid for state legislator. At 26, the love of his life, his sweetheart, who he thought he'd spend his whole life with, Ann Rutledge, dies. Another 3 years later, he lost another election to be the Speaker of the House in Illinois on the Representatives. He buried his own,child. I couldn't even imagine that pain.

Oh, it isn't over yet, at 39, Lincoln failed to become the Commissioner of the General Land of office in D.C. At 49, he was defeated in his try to be a U.S. senator, but even though he had many personal failures, many business failures and even more political failures, he just kept going. He was eventually elected to the Representatives, the U.S. Representatives. He drafted a bill at that point to try to end slavery. It didn't pass. By the age of 52, he is here at the Office of the President of the United States, the biggest and greatest office in the country, and possibly in the world.

Now, you can see his face on the $5 bill, and we all talk about him. I always say when I go into a presentation, I always talk about Abraham Lincoln. He is one of my favorite men in history. Everybody knows who he is. A few people know the 21st president, but everybody knows the 16th. Both guys did the same exact thing, around the same exact time. Why is one so known, the other is not? It's not what you do, it's how you do what you do. He stood for his morals and values. He fought through adversity, and he embraced the suck. He fought the struggle. He did not quit, and he kept going. He believed he knew his purpose, his calling in life , and he went and did it. For that, he will never die twice.

Now, listen you've heard some of my losses or read it, to say, and now you know about Abraham Lincoln's losses if you didn't. We know you have a loss too, but we know just because you have that loss, it doesn't mean you're lost. It's part of your journey. Don't miss it because of crap times. Triumph for them and use them to push you further. Nothing will hit as hard as life, but I will be damned if I don't try to hit back with the same impact and force. Make your life amazing in spite of the shit. Embrace the suck my friend.

Chapter 8

YOU ARE **YOUR** JOB.

"It's only when you take responsibility for your life, that you discover how powerful you truly are." – Allanah Hunt

I don't know how to make this as clear as it needs to be, but I will do my best. I had to make this a chapter, and it feels like this is a piece of every chapter. It's so important that it had to be its own as well. You are no one else's responsibility but yours. Your dreams are no one else's job, their focus, their number one, their energy, but yours. It's all up to you. That might not sound fair. You might not like it. It sounds hard and it is. It's going to be. If you want to live like the one-percenters, you're going to have to do what the one-percenters do, and that is tough. There are going to be days you don't want to do it, but you are your job. That's your responsibility. Heck, if you want to live like the 25%, you will have to do things that the 25% do. There is no way around this concept. There is no instant pill for greatness, dreams, or success. Will Smith says a line which I've already referenced in this book numerous times, "It's not your fault but it's your responsibility." Anything in your life could possibly not be your fault. There probably is blame to go around, but your life is your responsibility, all of it.

We talked in the other chapters about finding your passion, finding your why, and finding what makes your heart beat. That's called lighting your fuse by engaging the thought process to focus on what your calling is. So, now the mission is to ingrain as much of your life in that purpose, passion, and drive as you can. That's your fuse because it's not that hard when you love it. It's not that much of a pain in the ass when you love it. It's not that much of a nag when you love it. So light your fuse. Set it off. Set your soul ablaze. Light you up. Don't get anybody else to do it, don't ask anybody else to do it, don't look for anybody else to do it, and please, do not ever need someone else to do it.

Now, I'm not saying don't find motivation and inspiration and don't find people for your circle. You know how important that is. I'm not saying any of that, but you have to light your fuse. You have to keep it lit on the days where you're not going to want to. When things don't go your way, when it gets really hard, and when life hits you, it's going to be hard to keep that fuse lit. There are going to be days where you don't want to. Hell, there will be days when it's not burning, but you have to keep them small man. There can't be many days like that. They have to be very few and far in between, and its your job to make sure of it. You have to light your fuse. You have to get closer. You have to grow. You have to get better every day. Every day. I know that sounds ridiculous and impossible, but with that mindset, you're more than likely going to accomplish more, go further, and do the most. At the end, that's what keeps you going towards your destination, towards your goals, towards your mountaintops, and towards your pinnacle, whatever you want to call it. That's what keeps you going. That's what keeps you able to get up in the morning and get that ass in the gym when you want to stay in bed, when everybody else is in bed, when the covers are nice and warm the wind is cold as snow cone shavings outside.

You ask why am I doing this? Why? I wish someone told me this early and if it keeps your fuse lit, you will get further faster. It keeps you in the best shape physically and able to. If your goal is to love your family and to get to the top of any profession, you're going to need energy. You're going to need your body to support you doing it. Your body is your temple: it's your vessel. You have to keep it in good shape so it can go through the waters that you have to go through to get to where you want to get to. If you have a poor vessel, you probably won't make it far. You will probably have to stop to repair it often. Every time you have to stop to repair yourself, you are delaying the journey to your dream. You have to keep that fuse lit. It will make you know why you're getting up to do these things and why you're putting in extra hours. Why after you kiss your kids goodnight do you spend two more hours perfecting your craft and getting closer to your goals, dreams, and desires? Why? It's because that fuse is lit. You know what it means to you. You know how much it will mean to you. You know you have to be a part of it because it calls for you. You long for it. You get hyped just thinking about it.

Secondly, after you light that fuse, you have to hold yourself accountable. Are you getting to the gym? Are you working as hard as you can? Are you putting in the time? How can you do it better?

Listen, I said in your circle you want these three types of people around: the kind that build you up, the kind that lift you up, and the kind that check you to keep you up. I always say this to myself: check yourself so no one else has to. Am I really putting in the time? How can I be better at it? How can I do more of it? How can I do more of the better part of it and not just say I'm doing more work. Listen, there's 24 hours in a day. I know some people that say they work 16 of them. Yeah, but 4 or 5 of them, are kind of sluggish and slow and really not going all out on them. A couple other ones, are kind of doing it and going through the motions but not really going all out. Then, they go all out for like what, 2 hours? I know some people that say, "Listen, I only pursue and perfect my craft for 6 hours a day, but in that 6 hours, I'm going hard man. I'm going hard. I'm exhausting myself." Who do you think gets more done? The guy that did 16 hours, the guy that did 6 all out, or the guy that did 16 half-ass? Probably the 6 all out.

So it's not how much time are you putting in, it's how efficient the time is being put in. The only way you know that answer is by holding yourself accountable. You can tell me anything. You can tell the people around you anything. You can tell the people in your circle, in your family, your girl, or whoever it is, whatever you want, but you know you have to hold yourself accountable and say, "Listen, I have to do better." Right now I'm trying to eat better and trying to get on a better diet so I have longer energy and feel better. So that day when I eat that honey bun, I have to hold myself accountable and say, "Listen, you're doing that." You put that in your equation; no one's doing that to you. So next time, are you going to eat the honey bun? Listen, some days I eat the honey bun. Some days I don't, but I never say, "Oh, I did that because you know, people are stressing me out, so I just had to do it. Oh, I was just hungry, and I had to." No, no. I did it because I chose to do it. It's my choice to eat it like it's your choice to either get closer to your goals or further from them.

So, you have to be accountable, and you have to hold yourself accountable. And it's hard, believe me. Sometimes I curse myself out, like why? Like, stop it, leave me alone. When I'm talking to myself, people ask, "You okay?" I'm like, "Yeah, just telling myself how I'm messing up." Do you talk to yourself? I talk to myself all the time. Literally, like two days ago, as I'm doing this, someone in Walmart asked me if I was okay because I was talking to myself in an aisle. Sometimes I am the lunatic, but I'm always going to know exactly where I am and that it's my responsibility to get where I want to go.

The other part of the holding yourself accountable, is that you can only do that if you're telling yourself the truth. Like I said, you might lie to everybody else, but you know the truth. So, you have to be honest with yourself. You need to know where you started, where you are, and where you want to go. Sometimes I work with clients, and especially when I work with clients in the sports world where I kind of came from a little bit, a lot of times they'll tell me, "I really want to play professionally. I want to be a professional."

When they say that I always say, "That's a great goal."

Be honest with yourself. How close do you think you are to being that? Some of them are very honest, you know, "Far away, I've got a lot to do, I've got a lot to get better at."

"All right, cool. We're at a realistic point."

Others are like, "Pft, I could do it now." I'm like, "No, if you could you would be. If you did what it took to be a professional, you would be there." Let's not hold onto any excuses the will justify us from stopping the pursuit of goals.

It's that. Being honest with yourself will put you exactly where you are on that path. We talked about that earlier in the book. You're on this path. You're connecting dots. You're trying to figure out how to get this endgame from where you started, and if you're going through that, you're lying to yourself and saying you're at step 7 when you're at step 2. You're never going to get far because you're missing steps, and that's going to make you trip up. It will leave you missing dots to connect and creating a false path. It's like when you're running up the steps and you're trying to do 2 or 3 at a time, you kind of miss aim; you hit one of them, and it trips you up. You almost fall. You get a little nervous? Maybe that's just me. If you're not honest with yourself you're going to hit those steps and trip up, and it's going to keep you from getting to your destination for longer. If you're honest with yourself, you know exactly where you are so you know exactly where you have to go to get to where you want to get to. You'll get there faster and smoother. And you won't have those moments where it's the blame game, and "I'm the victim," and all that negative energy that comes from that.

So always be honest with yourself and hold yourself accountable.

All right, that fuse, I talked about lighting that fuse and then, I talked about keeping it lit and staying motivated. Man, people ask me about the toughest part of the journey, and it's because I've taken it a couple times with different businesses that I started and also my personal journey. I say the hardest part isn't to get motivated. The hardest part is to stay motivated. It's like being on top. The hardest part isn't getting on top. That's hard, don't get me wrong. It's extremely hard to be the best. It's even harder to stay there. You become the target. Also after you know the feeling of being on the mountaintop, some do not have the hunger to keep feeling it. For some, just getting there is enough, and the fall is coming fast because the hunger is gone. Your competition is the you of yesterday.

All right, please tell me you've seen Lebron James. He's an NBA player if you don't know. If you've been under a rock or just don't pay attention to anything sports or entertainment, or anything of that nature. Lebron James is one of the best that ever did it. He's won what, 3 championships in his 15 plus year career? For a decade, he's been the best. So, being the best is tough. Staying the best is even harder. Staying at that level, that pinnacle, that top, or that mountaintop, when multiple people are trying to knock you off of it … See sometimes people get confused, and they say, "This is my goal. I'm going towards it. That's it."

I say, Ah! All right, many other people are going towards that goal and fighting you for that top position. So even if you get to the top, you beat them all there, awesome. Great job. That's tough, and you should celebrate and enjoy that moment. Then as that next one goes, "Oh man, how do I stay here? How do I stay on top?"

Listen. My goal right now is to be the greatest motivational speaker and presenter out there that ever existed. That's my goal. I know it's hard. There's great people out there. There's people I idolize out there doing it right now, and I have to do it greater than them. I have to do it better than they do. So, I have to reach people more. I have to be able to motivate and inspire people more and for longer. And how am I going to do it? I'm going to do it through no longer just speaking but through books, videos, quotes, social media, guest appearances, podcasts, and all these things along the line, to be able to build up and build up, and build up, and build up, to be able to say, "Look, this is how I'm here. This is how I'm doing it." Then, "How do I keep doing it?" I keep doing it because I just don't want to get there and fall off. So it's to be the best for the longest. When you say, "What's your mountaintop?" That's it. Be the best for the longest.

People are like, "Oh, you should … Don't be in competition," or whatever, but it's not that I'm competing with them to do it. I'm competing with myself to make me that top of the line, that upper echelon, and master my craft. It wasn't that I did what I did, it's how I did what I did that made me stand apart and made me different and makes you different. You have to stay motivated!

I said this before in the book, and I'll say it again as well. I have 3 numbers written down on my nightstand., and I look at them every morning. This was one of my original why's. Remember my brother took his own life when I was a youngster, and then, one of my best friends took his own life in 2011. The first one is 22, the next one is 125, and the next one is 3,000. It's 22 people that serve or serve this country, U.S. of A., that I'm in, who take their own lives every day. 125 Americans take their own lives every day. 3,000 people in the world take their own lives every day.

My goal is to have those numbers become zero. Zero, zero, zero. That's my ultimate goal in my life, not my profession, not just my passion, but my life goal is to have those numbers be zero, zero, zero. That's what keeps me motivated. That's what keeps me going. That's why I know I can't stop. That's like when I don't want to get out of bed, I get out of bed. That's why when I don't want to do the extra video, I do the extra video. That's when I don't want to write another chapter, I write another chapter. That's when I don't want to edit more, I edit more. I look for ways to expand and grow more when I don't want to. I can think I'm okay at the level I'm at, or I can just coast for a little bit. That type of thought is where I fall behind.

What can you use to keep yourself motivated? What can you use to keep you going when the fuel is low? When the energy is not there and the feeling is not there? What do you have? What's your why? What's your life? Why? What's your career? Why? What's your profession? Why? What's your relationship? Why? You can have a why in these things and not just one ultimate. I think there is one ultimate. I think there should be one ultimate, but you can also have more. You can have more than one why. I mean, listen, some people just have one, but you don't just have to have one. There are a couple things that move you to that, where you won't stop. Well that's a why. It's not a rule that there's one and that's it. There is no "one and done." This isn't NCAA college basketball. You can have as many as you feel that deep down are real.

That's another thing. This is one of the things that really bothers me to my core. It actually pisses me off sometimes, when people tell me about these unwritten rules that someone else told them about, that someone else holds true so now you have to as well. It just expands, and then you make that a rule in your life. Listen. Make your own rules. I don't have just one why. I have multiple whys. They mean very much to me. I'm very passionate about them. There are not … Oh, then there are rules for everything, and I'm not sure I am following them. Make your own. In the speaking world, they say, "Listen. Don't give out too much content. You have to make them want to pay for something. You can't just keep giving things away." You're putting too many quotes, posts, and videos out a day. You're going to make people not want to listen to you. I know sometimes you make videos in hoodies and sweats. I see sometimes you do suits and that's great, but you have to do it all the time in suits because no one will take you seriously in that hoodie. These are things people have told me. If the best thing about me when I give a presentation is my outfit, I have failed you, and you shouldn't listen or waste the time to watch me then.

These rules people make up, don't go by them. Don't listen to them, and do not let them set limited beliefs for you. You probably have enough of your own. Make up your own rules. Live your life. Define your life. Define your rules. Define how you're going to go about your business. Now, I'm not saying people won't call you on them. You're going to have a reason why you picked your rules, and you can defend them. I don't care what I wear because what I wear will not be the impact. It will not be the importance. My message will be. So if I have a message that needs to be said whatever I'm wearing, I am going to say it and share it because that is what I am here for.

I had a buddy of mine make a pocket projector joke once because I had pens in my pocket, and I said, "Man, if that's the only thing you took from that video, you really didn't listen, or I did not do my part to bring the listener to the point." If my biggest knock when I do a presentation or a video is I have a pen in my pocket, I have a sweatshirt on or a T-shirt on, I am in a good place, but if its bringing attention to the message, well that's a serious issue. By the way, a couple of my favorite shirts are T-shirts, and there's something about a zip up hoodie that I feel at home in. So if you're expecting me not to wear those things, good luck. You'll probably see me in them more often than not. Don't get me wrong, there's some days that I'm in the office or doing things that I know I want to be in a different attire, or I want to be in a different attire because the mood is different. It's like a black tie event in my mind. I know the mood is different, and I know why I'm doing it. I'm not going off others' rules. I'm going off what I accept for the event, especially for some dinners, for fundraisers, or for great causes. I understand what they're doing, and even though that's the rule of the event, I accept that rule by going to it.

That's not the rule of my life, that it means every dinner I go to I have to wear a black tie, and it doesn't mean every time I go to my office I have to wear a suit coat. Make your own rules. Live your life. Listen, people are going to call you on it, people are going to question you on it, and people are going to try to bring you down. Just like crab pots, they don't want you to get out. Remind them, it's your life. However it goes, you're choosing how it goes. You're not going to place blame, you're going to take accountability for it, you're going to be the answer, and you're going to be honest to yourself about it. It doesn't change who you are and what you're going to do. Anyone that doesn't take you seriously because of your outfit, or because you have different rules, you probably didn't want to associate yourself with them anyway. So it's easy, move on and get on. At the end of the day, you have to choose your life.

I sit back and I think about the amount of people I've lost, and the time I lost them, and how I don't understand why I got so lucky to be here. I've done things that people have lost their lives doing, and I'm still here. I'm so thankful for the opportunity to still be here for my story to be continuing and for my dash to go longer because I know I don't necessarily deserve it or have earned it. It just is, but I know how much time I spent on jobs I didn't like, or didn't care about, or meant nothing to me, or sometimes made me miserable, or relationships that made me miserable. I think about the relationships that made me miss time and life, made me miss events, made me miss connections, which we all seek in our life. Everyone wants connection to something or someone bigger than just them.

I think about the time I wasted, and man, it really pisses me off. It makes me sad and angry. Don't waste your life. The good thing about it, it's all yours to pick. You choose it. Listen, if you are at the mall and you don't want to be? Leave. You're at a concert and you don't want to be? Leave. You're in a job you don't want to be in? Leave.

People say, "How do you say that with bills and everything else?" Oh, there are a million jobs. There's nothing worth being miserable over. I will say it again: there's nothing worth being miserable over. I'll tell you that a million times, and I'll tell you again if you need. There's nothing worth being miserable over. There's nothing worth it. Disease comes from dis-ease. I didn't make that up. You can google it. It has been around before me. You choose your life. Follow your heart. Make it worth it. Sometimes I wonder if my life is going to be some huge, embarrassing failure. Some guy that just crashed and burned. I think, man, if it is, it's going to be one hell of a song. It's going to be one hell of a movie. I'm going to go all out at it. They're not going to say it's because I didn't go, and I didn't go for the biggest and the baddest. What life are you choosing? It took me a while to choose, and in some areas I still have to. What about you? What areas in your life are you sitting here going, "I need to choose what I want in this. Is this really what I want? Is this really where I should be? Is this really where I should be going?"

Another thing I'll tell you, it's just life. You spend time wisely and accordingly to how you choose to. I had this 13-year fight. Well, it was for my daughter, and she's 16 now. She's amazing, a pain in the ass but amazing. I always wanted more with her, and sometimes when I'm following my own passion and profession, I think, " Should I be spending more time with her?" So I really try to do things with her to build our relationship. I talk to her about her video games she plays: she loves the Sims, and it drives me crazy. I talk to her about the weird, vampire-zombie books she reads that she's really into. I listen to the music she listens to, so we can talk about it and go to concerts, even though it gives me a headache most of the time. It's the little things where I know that I'll always hold those moments precious and hopefully, she'll be able to too. I was a teenager when my father died. There were many times now I think, "I should have spent more time with him." Many times I wish he was around. I know if I continue to spend this time and give these moments, she will not have to ask that question. I want her to have times to go to and say, "Wow, my dad loved me."

Are you spending time with the right people and doing the right things? I always say I'm a nerd. I like nerdy things. Sure, I played sports. I was pretty athletic. I once ran an under five-minute mile, not great, but good. I think, man, I like laser tag. I like playing video games. I like playing board games. I think how much time I avoided those things trying to be a cool person and didn't just do what I enjoy, and now, if it's not hurting someone else, and you're not hurting yourself, do what you enjoy, period. Spend time accordingly. Spend time with the right people. Spend time with the people you care about and you love and the people that care about you and love you.

When I was doing this, when I was trying to think of a person that I could talk about while doing it, it was pretty easy. As soon as I thought of the name and their life I was like, "Pft, this one's for this chapter." J. K. Rowling. If you don't know her, she's the author of the Harry Potter series. She had a strained relationship with her father. Her mother had an illness for most of her life. She failed and was rejected into Oxford University. She moved to Manchester with her boyfriend, and in 1999 at 25 years old, while on a four-hour delayed train, this idea of a wizard, a young wizard, popped into her head. She had this grand idea, and she just needed to turn it into something real. Right after that or at least shortly after that, her mother died just months later. You can imagine her mom dying made her upset and made her sad. It definitely was a setback.

After that, she moved to Portugal to teach English. She met a man and got married there and got pregnant. She gave birth to a little girl that was born in 1993. Her relationship with her husband wasn't a great one. There were reports of domestic violence and separation, and eventually divorce. She only had 3 chapters of Harry Potter then, and she was 38 years old. She then moved. She moved in with her sister actually. She thought she was a huge failure and thought she failed at everything she pretty much attempted. She was diagnosed with depression and was suicidal. It wasn't until 1995, that she finished Harry Potter. She had an agent, and they tried to get the book published. There was over a dozen publishing houses, and every single one rejected her idea. It wasn't until over a year later in 1996, when this tiny little publisher gave her a 1500 Euro-advance and green lighted her project. And then in 1997, literally 7 years after the idea of the young wizard, Harry Potter, the book was published, and then, we know the rest. In 2004, she became the first author to become a billionaire through writing books.

Talk about someone that was just herself. It was her job to be herself and to stay motivated; she was someone who held herself accountable and was honest with herself but then also, played by her own rules. She chose her life and spent her time the way she meant to and the way she wanted to. Of course, she could have easily given up at any time while growing up in the tough relationship with her father, while her mom was sick, or when her mom died. She could have given up when she was not able to get into college, when she was labeled depressed and suicidal, or when she was turned away from every major publishing house, or when she had to fight for 7 years to get this book out. Then 7 years after that, she was the first author to become a billionaire by selling books. Wow! If one can do it, anyone can do it. If anyone can do it, everyone can do it. Remember, the only person whose job it is to do it, is yours. Like I said, you are your job. Now get to it.

Chapter 9

GROW THROUGH IT

"A comfort place is a beautiful place, but nothing ever grows there."
– Unknown

You have to be willing to grow, adapt, and develop through your journey. We already talked about how we know situations are going to come. Trials and tribulations are going to be there on and off throughout your entire life. Life isn't going to be perfect. We're going to have a lot of battles, and the worst battles, the hardest battles, are going to be battles that you must take whatever life throws at you. We know that's going to happen. We don't need a fortune teller. We don't need to just hope it doesn't because it will not work that way. Just pray for the good times. We're going to have hard times. We talked about the L's of the journey and lessons and loss. Knowing that we're going to have them, do you let them make you or do you let them break you? Do you let them stop you or do you let them make you grow? I heard this once … I wish I can give credit to who said it. I heard it a million times, and I couldn't figure out who said it first. "You go through it or do you grow through it?" It is your choice, and it's all up to you.

How powerful is that? Do you go through your daily routines? Do you grow through your daily routines? Do you go through the hard parts in your life, in your journey, or do you grow through your hard parts in your journey? In everything, in your relationships, do you go through your daily relationships, or do you grow through them? Do you go through your daily grind at work, or do you grow through it? Do you go through the steps needed to get to your dreams, goals, desires, purpose, or calling, whatever you want to call it or name it, or do you grow through it? If you're just going through it, you'll never be living the best life you can live or be the best you. What a tragic way to go through this life. That's really just bullshit, and do not fall into that trap. Numerous people are hoping you will just go through it but not us. You have to grow through it to get to where you want to be and where we need you to be.

Remember when we are babies, we can't even hold our heads up. We poop all over ourselves, and we don't really say any words. We can't walk, and then all of a sudden, we turn ourselves over and sit up. We crawl, we walk, and we mumble things; then all of a sudden, we start saying words, start making sentences, and start making sense. I'll never forget when I was driving my daughter. I want to say she was like 4 years old. She was in the backseat and I was driving. It was a long drive between pick up and drop off. We were at a stoplight in a town or city in which I coached, and she said like a whole couple sentences that made complete sense. I just looked in the rear view mirror at her and was stunned  because it was the first time she did that. I also felt extremely proud and old at that moment when it was just a whole conversation that was 100% accurate.

I saw the growth she had and how far she had come ... I mean now I'm saying that and she's like a legit high honor roll student every quarter and semester in high school. She gets A's on finals and things that I'd never experienced when I was young, unless it was gym class. I think that's the only class I'd beat her in. I remember that day. I'll never forget it. I remember it because of her growth. We have to have those moments. Why do we think when we get older we stop growing, we stop improving, we stop getting better, and we stop getting to our destinations, rather than arriving? "Always going, right? Never arriving." I don't know who said that as well, but I heard it a million times since then. It's one of those things everybody says but it does not make it less true.

In order to grow, we have to be willing to learn. I always say every single person can teach you, and every single person can be taught by you. Even if we had some of the same experiences, how we went through them, our thought processes, and our actions could be different. We could have been enlightened differently, experienced the same thing differently, and learned different lessons from it.

That's why some people will go to a restaurant that you love and say it's horrible. You can't believe it. Why? It is because we experience the same thing differently. So always be a constant learner.

I remember talking to my mom, and my mom's an amazing woman and has lived an unbelievable life. I mean, in almost every aspect of life, you can look and just be in awe of what she did, what she went through, and how she did it. I remember sitting there talking to this woman who has 2 doctorates, raised 6 kids, and went through a hell of trials and tribulations from different illnesses to tragedies in life.

When I said, "Mom, what do you think is one word to describe you?" She said, "Learner." I was stunned. I said, "What?" She goes, "a constant learner."

What she said to me, stuck with me. She has accomplished so much in business: from being an entrepreneur, from being a small business owner, to working her way up to directing the whole state division for mental health, and so much more. This woman, who has done it in every aspect of life, sat there and said, "I'm a constant learner. I just want to keep learning. I want to keep taking things from people, from books, from situations, or anything I can. I just want to learn from it."

We grow through knowledge. We grow through understanding. We grow through developing. When you sit there and go, "Oh, this person is talking to me, but I'm more worried about what I want to say back," rather than listening to what they're saying or feeling, or what they went through, and how they went through it. Which one do you think would help you the most and not just make you feel better? When you're talking about anything are you listening to learn or listening to be right?

I'm just trying to say what I wanted to say or the points I already developed that I knew I was going to win with, rather than growing as a fan or as a person by listening to the other side of the coin just because it wasn't my side. It's about the will to listen, being willing to learn, and to be willing to soak in information rather than just getting your point across. I'm not saying just take it, or you have to take it all and not say your peace, thoughts, or opinion.

No. You do not have to believe and agree with everything said to you. I'm not saying that at all but take it in. See, the worst part of a conversation are things I will disagree with. If that's the worst part, awesome, I don't have to take it, but I'm going to listen.

Even if I don't agree, I'm going to learn their point of view. I'm going to learn where they're coming from. Even then I have a platform to be able to say, "Listen, I understand what you're saying and the way you're looking at it, but you also can look at it this way from this angle." It's not preparing a rebuttal; it's understanding how the two views differ and how I can see it from their side. Hopefully, I can speak so they can understand that from my side, but you have to learn to be able to do this. To be able to expand where you are right now, you have to learn how to go to the next level, or should I say grow to the next level?

I have been saying this the last couple days, and it's really been sticking in my head because I've been listening to people tell me about different goals that they have for the new year.

It's this idea where it's, "Oh, I'm just going jump to this spot in this career or this profession, or I'm just changing this to sound good for the new year."

I always ask, "Are you prepared for that? Do you know how to do that? Are you ready for that kind of move because it's a big move?"

"Oh, yeah, yeah. I'm ready. I'm ready."

All right. That's very convincing, but are you really ready for what you're doing? Are you prepared? Have you looked into it? Have you grown into the person that can achieve this, or are you just saying it because it is almost a new year? Are you motivated to be better or motivated because of the moment. One will fade as the days will, and the other will be deep- rooted inside of you.

Now, I understand the experience part and it matters, but it still always drives me crazy because people will say, "You need 4 years experience."

"I can't get this job until I get 4 years experience. So, how can I ever get the job?"

No, I get it but it's infuriating, and it drives me crazy on applications. I really don't ever ask for you to need any certain amount of experience. When we're looking for people to join our team, it's more about what kind of person you are to your core. What vibes do you send? What morals and values do you hold dear and so on? If you have any experience, that's awesome, but if you don't, it's okay. What kind of person are you? Are you the kind of person that we want to be around and that we want our team around? That's something that's so important to us that our hearts will be protected by this type of person.

So, I understand the idea of what we need, but how can we get experience if we don't do it? So go do it! I know that is frightening even for me when I started things without any experience. For example, when I walked into my first presentation room or the first motivational speech I gave, I never did one before and was all kinds of freaking out inside, of course. I prepared for that moment over and over again. Man, I had it in my mind every time they were not going to clap. Thank the Lord they did every time we thought we were going to get a boo or even worse silence. Every time I was thinking that moment that I really wanted them to process what I said and how I meant it. I had it matched to a T, so when it happened, I already saw it. I was ready. So it might have been the first time I gave my speech but I really gave it hundreds of times in my head already before that day. That's how you get experience without having it.

I did it a million times, even though I didn't do it once yet. Are you going to be prepared,? Are you going to learn how to do the task so you can do the task? Preparation and execution is key. Do you want to be in the 1 percent? You have to do what the 1 percent does. What the 1 percent does is they master their craft. When I say it, I mean it. They master their craft. They're sitting there and hammering at their craft. They say it takes 10,000 hours to master something, 10,000 hours. 10,000 hours to master a craft, think about that.

How many of you have spent 10,000 plus hours to master your craft to that level? I'm not talking about achieving perfection but rather a mastery level. Yeah, right, not many.

Probably a ton of people will try to find make-believe hours they spent and maybe add this in, "I am probably close."

Sure you are. LOL.

How many of you are really trying to perfect your craft, what you're doing, or even more important, your calling? Listen I don't care what you do, I care how you do it. That's what is going to set you apart. Most people know Abraham Lincoln, but few people know who the 21st President was. They were both presidents!!!

Remember I said it in Chapter 1, it's not what you do, it's how you do what you do that matters. When I go into my favorite coffee shop and there are people that I know behind the counter that I'm not excited to see they're working, I try to go to the people that I'm really excited to see when they're working. Why? It's because how they do what they do matters. They mastered their craft, or they've done enough to make it appear like they're on their way to perfecting their craft and that gives me confidence in them and also puts a smile on my face. Whenever I get smiles, I take them. I'm a smile hoarder; I take them all and look for any chance to plaster one on my face.

I'm sure everybody can relate. Whether it's the grocery store you go in, the corner store you go in, or the gas station you go in regularly, you've built a rapport with some people and formed a connection with some people that work there, and you try to go to them. When you go to the bank you go to, you try to go to a certain teller. It is because you've built that connection. You've built that rapport because the way they do their craft. I am sure you probably know their name, and I'm sure you probably don't know the person's name at the register next to them.

Why? It is because the way they do their craft. They've worked on it; they've worked on that mastery level. They're working on perfecting it, and they do it better. Of course, you want the person that does it better. You want to be treated better, and you want to go through the process quicker, smoother, and better. We all want the best, and that isn't a bad thing. So master your craft. Notice I'm not asking you to spend every waking hour on it or every moment you are awake to do it.

Are you finding time to do it daily? Are you finding time to share it, to get feedback from it, to see that you're growing and getting better? Are you doing it enough so that you're not being stagnant because stagnation is a killer? There's no such thing as staying still. If you're staying still, you're falling behind. So, are you moving forward? The key is to keep moving forward, always keep learning, always keep developing, always keep perfecting your craft, and always try to keep achieving a mastery level in everything you do. Always have a goal, and at the end of that goal, have another goal. They are the stepping stones to where you want to go.

The mountain top is great. Believe me, I've been there in certain aspects of my life. You know what happens when I get there? It's a beautiful view, and I look over and sooner or later see another mountain and start climbing. Always becoming, never arriving. I always tell the story about your masterpiece, and we will talk about it before the end of this book. Paint your masterpiece!

I always say this, and I'll say it again in this chapter, I never want to see my masterpiece because I want to keep developing it all the way until I'm gone. I don't care if I'm 115 years old. If I'm 115 years old, I hope I'm still painting my masterpiece when I go. At the end they'll put it together and go, "Whoa, he never really got to see all he did, but Wow, look at the impact he made. Look at the people he helped. Look how he tried to spread positivity and move everybody forward. It wasn't a selfish life: it was a life about others, about service. He wanted us all to make it, and look, this is how he tried to help. This is how he tried to do it. Look how he got better at his presentations and his speaking. Look how his books got better."

I look at my first book now and laugh at it, and this only my second one. Don't get me wrong, I think it serves its purpose. I think it's a good read, I mean, you can do it. It's an easy one. Actually, it's more of a workbook. You write your pieces as you go, but whatever, shameless plug.

I look at it and laugh at some of the mistakes I made and some of the areas I added in, the way I run all over the place, and it's laughable. It's funny to me ... now. That's not me belittling my work, but it's me growing.

I was talking to someone about this book, and they asked me how the chapters look. I said, "You know what's funny? The chapters are double, triple, and quadrupled in the length of the chapters of my first book."

They said, "That's growth."

What's crazy is the first book I thought was going to be easier because it was just life stories and life lessons that we all can probably relate to, and we all have our own. That was the point of the book: your story. It wasn't necessarily about mine; I shared mine freely to be able to make you feel more comfortable to share yours, but it's about growing and moving forward because that's how you keep developing. If I stay still, I'm not growing, I'm not getting better. I'm not improving. I'm not the best me. The best me today is the worst me tomorrow.

The goal is to be the best me, the best me possible living the best life possible. I hope that's for you too. I want you to be the best you living the best life for you. That's how we all move forward. That's how we push the flag farther down the field for the next generation to carry it further, and the next generation to carry it further, and the next generation to carry it further. Remember I talked about those mountaintops, and it's very easy. We've seen it. We've seen teams win championships and then fall off the face of the earth. We've seen big businesses pop up and challenge the status quo and then disappear almost as quickly as they came. We've seen it and what happens is, they rest. I talked about this in earlier chapters: it's easier to become a champion rather than to stay a champion. Why? People rest on success. When you get to that mountaintop, if you don't see another one and if you're not willing to create another mountain, you know what happens. People start climbing down. People stay put and if you are not going forward, you are going backwards.

Don't climb down the mountain. See another one and go conquer it. See another one and go get it. Build another one and go climb it. Make one yourself and devise your plan on how you're going to get to the top again, but do not rest on success. Do not take that as a glory path. That's one but who's to say you can't have more. Who's to say there are no more out there for you, that you're not capable of making a bigger impact, a bigger crater, a bigger feeling, a bigger family or circle , or whatever you want to call it?

Don't limit your impact, and don't limit who you touch with your life message, your purpose, or your calling. Don't limit the people that can be affected by your masterpiece, hopefully in a positive way. Why limit yourself or anybody else by resting with success? I get asked this question often in the small businesses I have. "Why do you change things, and why do you branch out and do different things when certain things you do really work.?"

I say this, "I'm not going to rest on that success because sooner or later that won't work." When it doesn't work, what happens?

Look at businesses that have failed that had a great product or did an amazing thing. Look at Toys R Us. Toys R Us was an amazing business, but it rested on its success. It didn't keep growing and developing, and it didn't grow when the internet grew. It's online platform didn't grow. It's capabilities and it's shipping didn't advance. Nothing changed while everything else was changing. If you're not changing with everything else, you're losing. Don't lose. Change with time. Toys R Us isn't the only one. Blockbuster is another, right? You can go through a bunch of businesses, dozens and dozens that now do not exist or are on their way out even though they were great. Many were huge businesses that you probably remember that were in your area or community that you probably used yourself.

Why? All of a sudden people didn't watch movies? People didn't buy toys for their kids? No, they did, but people developed easier ways to do it while the other companies wouldn't move with the tide and fought it. They found more time efficient and more cost efficient ways of doing it and others didn't. When you talk about time, life is measured in it. That's how important time is. The most precious resource on earth is time. So if you give me a way where I can save it, I'm interested. What happened was those companies didn't give you a way and other people did. They no longer exist really because of it.

So don't rest on your success. You never know when the next turn is coming. The economy, the stock market, it's all a cycle. You have to be prepared for the next part. You have to be prepared like Jim Rohn used to say, "The fall's right before the winter." It's not a coincidence. You have to be prepared for the winter. You have to be prepared for the fall. You have to be prepared for what's next. So do not rest, and do not stop on your success; I hope you have plenty of it. Celebrate it and keep it moving.

The only way to have plenty of it is not stopping when you achieve it or receive it. Keep pushing through. There's another mountain. Find it or build it yourself, but don't rest on success. Really what I'm saying is to keep evolving, keep developing, and keep growing. If you're doing that, you're not even going to notice the hurdles, stumbling blocks, or cliffs that other people or businesses are going over because they're not willing to do the work over and over again.

The developing, the growing, and the pain, self-growth is one of them for sure. People always talk about personal growth. It's one of the most painful things to go through because like we talk about, you have to acknowledge where you are, all your shortcomings, and all your mistakes to be able to go to the next one and grow from there and move from there. Personal growth is extremely tough, and it's extremely painful. It creates really bad moments sometimes, but it's worth it because that's the only way to keep moving forward and to keep evolving into the best you, living your best life.

I don't care if it's your business, yourself, your relationships, or your career. Whatever state you're talking about that you're doing it in whether it's spiritual or emotional, keep evolving. Keep developing it and keep pushing forward. It's the only way to get to your best you. I smile sometimes when people say, "I'm living the best life."

I want to say, I don't want to be Debbie Downer, "You're living the best life possible, you could possibly be right now. How do you keep it that way? What can you do to keep it the best? Keep watering it for it to grow."

So even the people that are saying, "Listen, I'm on top of my game." All right, good. Congrats, I'm happy for you. How do you stay there? How do you keep evolving to stay at the top of you? What do you do? When I thought about "Growing through it," there were so many people that you can pick out for this one. There are so many people I could use as an example rather than writing anything I went through, but you know me, I always will throw some of my own stories in there.

When I think back, I think about Henry Ford. When Henry Ford was trying to build the Ford company, Ford Motor Company, he became one of the richest and most famous individuals on the planet. When he was trying to develop it and plan it out, they asked, "Did you ask people what they wanted"?

He said, "No. They would have told me they wanted a faster horses."

Wow, think about that, being willing to be all by yourself with this idea and concept that no one's even grasping around you. Not only that but he was also trying to put this into motion and make this dream into a reality.

Henry Ford

Ford didn't even become an engineer until he was 28 years old, almost 30 years old. He worked for Edison, of course. Until he was 30, he didn't even become a chief engineer. It wasn't until 35 that he designed and built a self-propelled vehicle and showed it off to people. A year later he developed his company. His company failed because they couldn't pay back a loan that they actually took from none other than the Dodge brothers because the inefficiency of the vehicle that he created. Of course, that had to be a heavy hit for him and one heck of a life lesson.

He got another chance with all that pressure and with all that doubt, and then guess what? It flopped again. It wasn't until he was over 40 years old, and after multiple failures, he got another shot. He made the Ford Motor Company and became one of the greatest story's of an individual's success in the biggest way possible we've ever seen: everybody knows Ford.

He had to grow through all those setbacks, all those failures, and all those disappointments. Starting later in life, He started at 28 rather than 22 like most engineers coming out of school. He had every reason to quit, and he had every reason to stop. He had every reason not to move forward, and he had every reason not to perfect his craft. He had every reason not to learn more. He had every reason to not evolve and he did, and by doing it, he will probably live forever. Because I don't know when we'll stop saying the name Ford, but it's probably a long way away. It's already lasted a long time.

That's how you do it. Listen, I was born without the ability to hear. I didn't get that ability until I was 3 years old. I couldn't talk at the age that normal kids could talk. I was a mess up in school. I failed third grade because I couldn't read with the other kids. In fifth grade I had to go back to third grade for reading classes. That was their solution.

In middle school they said to my parents to take me out of school and teach me a trade because it was the only chance I had to be successful. Funny story. They said the same thing to my mom when she was a kid, her parents. In high school they said I'd be dead or in jail by 21. People have doubted me. I have failed multiple times. I've been told I'd never be anything, and at any moment, I could have let that stop me. That could of become my built-in excuse. I am thankful every day for the parents I had that would not let me

… They wouldn't let that define me. They wouldn't let that make me. They wouldn't let me believe it. They wouldn't let me stop.

I had to keep learning; I had to keep evolving. I had to keep mastering my craft. I had to keep moving forward, and when I succeeded at certain things, they wouldn't let me rest on that. What was next, that's awesome? Chapter done. Celebrate the next day. Where are we going? How are we moving forward? What's the next success? Keep evolving as a person.

Think about the kid I just described. He bombed out of college multiple times. I love ET because every time he says it took him 12 years to get a 4 year degree, I'm like, "ET, I got you beat. It took me like 16 years to get a 4 year degree. It's sad but true. It actually took me longer. It took me 18 years to get a 4 year degree. Man, I'm sure it would've been easier to quit. It wouldn't have been better, but it sure would have been easier.

To think that guy, that guy who coached YMCA basketball became a college coach. That guy that got fired from dishwashing went on to open his own businesses. That guy that was a selfish prick became the Executive Director of a foundation that changes thousands of lives a year. That guy that couldn't read at a fifth grade level wrote books. That guy that couldn't speak when everybody else could speak, gives presentations for hours and releases videos. This isn't tooting my own horn. I'm telling you that if I can do this, you can do anything you want to do.

I mean anything, You can do anything that sets your soul on fire, anything that you're willing to battle for, and anything that you're willing to just keep pushing and keep moving towards. You can do anything. I promise you. If anyone can, all of us can. If anyone can, everyone can. I'm not special. We all have this within us, that greatness ready to be tapped. So I plead with you, tap into your greatness. Man, let us all see it. It's going to be awesome. I can't wait.

Chapter 10

SEE IT TILL IT'S REAL

"The Key to effective visualization is to create the most detailed, clear and vivid a picture to focus on." – George St. Pierre

See it, even when it's not there. I know that sounds crazy, right? "See it when it's not there"? I mean, literally, that is a sign that something could be seriously wrong if you're seeing things that aren't there. People have been put into safe rooms over saying those exact words. It also could be a sign that something's extremely right, and you are on the right path.

Follow me. I know this might be tough, but its so helpful to achieve whatever goals you have. There's this thing called the Law of Attraction. If you have not heard of it, please google it. The short definition is if you think about something long and hard, you will find a way to get it. The problem is it works for good and bad so choose positive thoughts. There are many different phrases you can use for this, but the concept is true and is clear. First, you have to see something, and you have to believe it before you can go get it. There are many people that have never seen the car that they want, the house that they want, the career that they want, the life that they want, the love that they want, the money that they want, the family that they want, or the kind of friends that they want, so they don't know it exists and can't really want it. If you can not see it, how could you ever know the way to get it?

I've been lucky enough to work with some of the most amazing youths there are in coaching because before I understood what coaching individuals was, I coached basketball. I thought that's how you coached, and that's how you can reach people to achieve bigger and better things than you or they thought possible. Unfortunately, some of them lived in and through horrible situations way too young. When I would talk to them about going to college or when I would talk to them about getting jobs, they would say, "Listen, we have a family business. Everyone in my family deals drugs. Why wouldn't I ... How am I not supposed to do that? Why wouldn't that be me and my life?" It would happen over and over again. It would break my heart and move me to the brink of tears every time. To see that as your only option for the rest of your life is heart wrenching to say the least. I would have to convince them that they could see a better life and not only that they could see it, but know they could be those other things that aren't necessarily right next to them. Take the blinders off. Close your eyes and picture the life you want. Envision it, all of it. Do not let others' limitations set your boundaries. Their path does not have to determine yours.

And like I said, have a vision … When they say, "Have a vision of your life," I think that's too broad. Of course you're supposed to have a vision of your life, but what does your life entail? What comes with it? A career? Love? Relationships, all different types? Family, friends, relationships? Career or profession? Emotionally, how do you want to be? Spiritually, how do you want to be? How do you want to be in the community? What kind of legacy do you want to leave? What kind of impact do you want to make? In what field do you want to make it? These questions should go on and get deeper as they go for you to truly have a better understanding of you.

There are so many visions you should have about your life and your self. When you put these all together, the kind of person you are is shown to you. When you put these together, that's the life you want to lead deep down. That's your goal, and that's your vision of you in your life. You have to have visions of all of it, and I mean crystal-clear visions. Literally, take some time right now. Put this book down, and put the highlighter down. Clear your mind and think about the life you want in every aspect. Start with yourself: "What kind of person do I want to be? How do I want to be remembered? What do I want my obituary to say?" We do this exercise where you write your own obituary. How do you want people to remember you? What do you want your legacy to be and your impact that you made? What is it? Get personal with yourself. Be willing to know yourself at a deepest levels you can. That's the only way to truly love yourself, but then it's so much more. What kind of marriage do you want, or do you even want a marriage? What kind of relationship do you want that's intimate at any level? What kind of friendships do you want? Do you want a hundred million friendships, or do you want a couple real thorough, loyal, and truest-tested friends? Do you want two dozen good friends? I mean, what kind of friend? What are you looking for as a friend, and what kind of friend are you going to be? What levels are you setting that will make you say, "This is an acceptable level of this friendship, this love, this career, this job, this profession, this emotional state, or whatever it is?"

What kind of family are you going to have? What kind of family are you going to be? Are you going to do family trips, or are you going to do smaller things but more often? Or are you going to do both? And when you do family trips, what kind of trips do you want them to be? Relaxed, casual, beach, shorts, and sun? Do you want them to be educational like museums or want to learn about historical sites? What kind of car do you want to drive? Why do you want to drive it? What kind of house do you want? How many bedrooms? How many bathrooms? What kind of layout? Do you want a porch? What kind of porch? How big of a porch? Do you want a pool? What kind of pool? What is the stonework around the pool going to look like? I mean, think about everything to the detail. Draw out your life, your goals, and your aspirations. Have this vision that's so crystal clear that you know every second of it and if you're getting closer to it or farther from it, how to correct it.

I remember one of the first speeches I ever gave. I say that like it was a hundred years ago or something. It wasn't. I said, "Every day, you walk out in the street, and your goals and everything you want is at the end of one side. The other side gets you further and further away, and every decision you make during that day is going to either get you closer to it or farther from it." That's as true as it was then as it is now. Are you getting closer to that vision you've seen? If not, why? If not, what can you do to get closer to it? What kind of choices are you going to make to get closer to it? What kind of commitments in your life are you going to make to get closer to it? What kind of standards are you going to set that you won't allow yourself to go below, so you know you're getting closer to it? What kind of people are you willing to give that time to, and what kind of people are you not willing to give that time to? Then stick to it!

The more you do the things that help you, the closer you'll get to having all these visions you have come together and form your life. Have goals. Have a ton of goals. Goals are great, but also, be aware that you have to grow as you try to achieve more. Like we talked about previously: achievement stones. You need to see the mountaintop, and you need to know what your perfect is. You need to know what your goal is, what your mountaintop is, and what your ultimate prize is. You need to see where you are, and you need to set achievement stones along the way. Achievement stones are easy to set and easy to keep track of for progress. For example, you want to lose 50 pounds? All right, start working out, start eating better, and maybe start a regular diet. Don't start dieting but eat a regular diet. Lower your calorie intake every day, and you'll lose weight. All right, if you lose 5 pounds, that's an achievement. Nice, celebrate that. I'm not saying go out and eat cake, but celebrate that and reward yourself. Celebrate yourself for getting a step closer. If you lose 10 pounds, nice, there you go, another achievement. If you lose 20 pounds, another achievement. 25 pounds, you're halfway there, so celebrate it. Keep setting these marks and crushing them. Along the way celebrate the heck out of them.

Set these achievement stones, and listen, when you achieve things or when you're getting closer to these goals, celebrate it. Enjoy it. The journey is supposed to be the best part. It can't be the best part if it's just utter torture because there are going to be times where it's just hard, where you struggle, where it's a sacrifice, and where it's a pain in the ass. It's going to be a pain in the ass, so you have to make it a worthwhile pain in the ass. So when you're achieving it, and going through all the hard stuff, and dedicating yourself to it, and you are getting closer, and you see it by the scale or by how you feel, no matter how you judge it, enjoy it. Take it in and embrace it. Don't get stuck on it but definitely, reward good work. The mind will react in a positive way and want more of it. Never be too cool to train yourself, to adopt, or to adjust. It's all part of it.

I love this phrase: I've been doing it for years, and now it's been so long, I forget where it was, but it was about coaching teams when you win or lose. If you won, you had 24 hours to celebrate, and if you lost, you had 24 hours to be pissed off and then it was next. What's next or on to the next one? I have taken that mindset into how to achieve goals, getting achievement stones, getting closer to it, and making progress. When you make progress, you're winning, so enjoy it, celebrate it, and acknowledge it. I literally can not say it enough. Get that feeling of when you're achieving something. The feeling you get is rewarding, and the feeling you get is love. It's this amazing excitement in you. If you don't get that, what do you get from winning? Just winning? It's supposed to be bigger than that. It's supposed to be greater than that. Life is about more than that. Do not let the life-suckers ruin your time on this earth or throughout your life.

Set achievement stones, and celebrate along the way. Your achievement stones will set your path, this path to this mountaintop you have. You're going to have mountaintops in all the areas we talked about: remember, relationships, business, life, family, love, friends and many more. You will have all these kinds of steps throughout your journey. Even you personally, what do you want your look to be? I'm not talking about the clothes you wear. That too, if you want. What kind of shape do you want to be in? What kind of personality do you want to have? What kind of person do you want to be? What kind of legacy do you want to leave? What kind of impact are you going to make? They can go on and on, but ask the ones that you need to hear.

You have all these different mountaintops and all these achievement stones on the way, and that's the path to the top. That's your path, and that's no one else's path. Listen, don't be like, "Well, this is how this person did it, so I have to do it this way." No, no, it is never like that.

You're your own person not some BS pyramid scheme. Know it is bigger than that. I know plenty of people in the speaking business that have started in classrooms and in a decade worked themself up to the big stage, and I know people that have created the big stages themselves in a couple years and stood on it. Heck, they owned it. Everyone's path is their own. Find your path, and go on that road. Don't try to go on someone else's path; make your path because that's what's best for you. That's what gives you the best chance to succeed. That is what will teach you what you need to know to grow into the person that can accomplish what you want to do in this life. Your path will give you what you need to make it.

Here's the problem. We're all looking at … Oh, physical fitness. It's the must thing. There's a million people out there, and they look amazing. They look like they're really good at what they do. Trust me, they look like a real product carved out of stone. They tell you how they did it, and I always sit there and go, "That worked for you. The job is not what worked for you. The job is what works for them." So I don't sit here in that kind of shape, but I believe if I say, "Find your path and what works for you to be able to do this," would be better than me telling you how I did it and how I ran businesses. You have to run your businesses not me. Advice is great and learning from others is key, but don't take anyone else's path but yours.

Now, there are some things that we know will not work for you. Spending more than you make is bad, we all know that. Like, that's a bad business move. I'm not talking about that, I'm talking about how you run your business, how you run the management part of it, how you set the levels up of it, how you decide to be with your employees, and how you try to be with your customers. That's all on you, like how many customers do you want? How many employees do you want? How do you actually want to sell products? These are all up to you. What products do you want to sell? This is all up to you. This isn't up to anybody else, and don't let it be. Make your path along that mountain and go on it. Make your path because at the end, it's not going to be that you follow someone's path. It's going to be, "I made it my way." You decide your values and your culture.

You're going to have to because that guy, anybody, including myself, that's telling you some path to follow isn't going to be there for when you sink or swim. They're not going to be there to say, "Oh, come on now. Hold on, just keep going this way." And if you fail, they're not going to say it was because of their guidance. So, be careful with what anyone else tells you. Hell, be careful with what I tell you you should do. You should do whatever sets your soul on fire, whatever makes your soul burn in flames for it, whatever makes your heart leap, and whatever makes you want to go so bad that no one can stop you. When you see that way, you take that way, and you go all out for it. You do everything you can, so at the end, you laid all your chips on the table and went all in on your hand, your life, your goals, and your dreams to live it the best way, by being the best you. Whatever that is and however that breaks down, that's worth it. That's a success. Define your own success and live for it.

Here's this funny thing with success. Success is funny because success is whatever you make it. There is no one certain way to define that word. It is different for each and everyone of us. No one else can tell you what your success is nor should you let them try. You say what your success is. I used to tell my teams, "Every team has their own max out." Some teams I coached, we could have won championships. Some teams I coached, we did win championships. Some teams I coached did not have it in the cards. It wasn't that team's success rate, and it wasn't a championship for them. That team's success story was something different: it was theirs.

One of the most successful teams I ever had won 11 games and lost 9 of them. I have had teams win 15 and 14 games in a season, but the 11-win team was the best. This team lost 3 of its starting players at the beginning of the school year due to non-academic and non-injury-related situations, lost 3 of 5 starters, and the best player talent-wise on the team and maybe in the state. He went on to play overseas professionally. They lost 3 of them at the beginning of the year and had to figure out their identity on the fly. While other teams were making progress, we were trying to figure out the team it was going to be. I always say this was my most successful team because the way they maxed out. They went past the max out line. They went beyond what their success should have been or what outside expectations said it would be because of what they went through. Then they had to withstand injuries and other trials and tribulations that came along with a season like every season does. This team was so mentally and physically tough, I still admire them to this very day. I get moved to tears just thinking of their heart.

Not only did they do it, they went on to have a winning record, something that school only experienced one other time in any sport, period. It was the year before basketball team, that same basketball team that lost their 3 starters and went on to win 11 games and finished with a winning record. Most people don't even know that. People always talk to me about state tournament teams, the teams that won conferences or teams that won tournaments, and think those are the teams that I'm going to have the biggest accolades to talk about. When they say, "What team is the one that sticks out to you the most?" I'll always say that 11 and 9 team because they had every reason to quit and didn't. They had every reason and every excuse to pack it in and say, "This is to blame, and this is to blame. This is to blame, and it was nothing that we could control." They didn't. They maxed out.

We all have max outs. Now, don't believe what other people's limitations or doubts they put on you. Don't believe what story they tell you is yours; that's all theirs. You make your story. You create it, and you draw up your success. Remember when I said, "Have your vision. Have your map," and I went through all these things? I didn't say this one word because I wanted to save it for this point. You get to say what success is to you. You get to determine what your mountaintops are and where your mountaintops are. You get to determine what your perfect utopia is and what your grand success is in every aspect of your life.

No one can tell you if you're successful other than you. They didn't live your life, nor do they know every twist and turn about it. They know what they want to see of it. That's why I could take the same person and get two different opinions on them. I tell people all the time, I say, "My mom thinks I'm the most amazing person on earth. My ex thinks I'm the worst. I imagine I'm somewhere in the middle." I can take the same person and show you someone that likes them, someone that probably dislikes them, someone that loves them, and someone that probably hates them. Same person. Why? It's because we get to draw up what everyone else is and what everything is to us.

So if you can do that with people, you can do that with success. You can do that with your life, with every aspect. You can do that with your mountaintop. You can do that to your path. You can do that to every goal you have and everything else you think and know and love in life. You can do that to every aspect of your life. It's for you to decide and no one else. Do not let them.

Stop trying to give your power to other people. Your life is your power. This moment is your power. The next moment is your power. Your success, what is success to you? Your power. What's your career or profession, your calling, your purpose, and your passion? It's your call, all your call. You decide. What's your significant other going to be? You decide. What's your family going to be? You decide. What's your friends going to look like? You decide. You decide all of it. And when I say "look like," I don't mean appearance. What do they look like to you? Do they come over to your place and watch football with you? Do they just BS with you but are never really there for you? Listen, I have people. They tell me they love me. I have people that tell me they love me that live down the street from me that I rarely ever see. I have people that live across the country that text me, call me, or FaceTime me almost daily.

I mean, everything's what you want it to be. What do you accept it to be? What do you want your friends to look like? What kind of friendships do you want to have? It's every aspect of life. You have to envision it; you have to see what success is. You have to see what success is in all these different areas and in all these different fields, and you get to pick. What is it? That's some power right there. Don't give anyone else that power that's yours. You are the master of you.

The person I want to bring up in this one is someone that you probably have seen Will Smith play, named Chris Gardner, from *The Pursuit of Happiness*. We all know the movie, hopefully. If you haven't, you should see it, like now. He had a rough upbringing to say the least. Their stepfather was abusive to him, his mother, and his siblings. He was in and out of the foster care system which we all know can break a kid from ever believing in something great. He was married but had a child with a different woman through an affair. The outside ridicule was only second to self-talk at times. He worked at a research lab, and you could say it didn't pay great. He couldn't support a whole family doing it, so he made this bold decision that he was going to go sell equipment, medical equipment. And man, no one was really buying or even interested in what he was pushing. He went back to college and dropped out again like he did other times. Old mindset and old behaviors will always equal repeated results.

At one point, he was remembered saying that he was looked at as very ordinary or below ordinary when it comes to intellect. He was known as a failure and reminded of it often. We all know how the movie turned out. He was homeless but didn't end up homeless. He was broke but didn't end up broke. He was down and out, ran out, and made to believe he was little but wasn't. He went on to become a muti-millionaire working towards a billion. It was a huge success story when at one point, it was believed not to be. He was made to believe he would be less than most. He had every reason to believe them, but there was something inside that wouldn't let him quit fighting. Do you have that?

His vision was never his story, and even now, he is still seeing something bigger. His vision was always something bigger, and that's how he got through all those moments, when many would quit, because his vision wasn't that. He knew all he had to do was work for it, and he would get it. He had to keep working for it, and he had to see it. He had to go for what he saw. He had to see that mountaintop; he had to make his path. It wasn't like anyone else's path, it was his path. His path was rough, man, and his path made him want to quit himself. He said, "I wanted to quit." He was sleeping on bathroom floors, staying in shelters, finding any way to protect his kid and give him a chance, and have a chance to live the life in which he visioned.

Now, he was just an ordinary man. He wasn't born with a silver spoon and didn't have extra opportunities, but he took advantage of what he had which was very little and made the most of it. He maxed out. His vision, you ask him, he'd probably say it's not even close. That's just a guess of mine though because his vision's probably not done yet because as you grow, your vision grows. As you get higher, you see more. So as you're climbing that mountain and going on your path, you're going to see more and more the higher you get because a midget standing on the shoulders of a giant sees farther than the giant.

What do you see? What do you see now? In every aspect of your life, what do you see? If I ever believed people, if I believed the setbacks I had, if I believed the naysayers, if I believed the people that told me I wouldn't be in there, I wouldn't be here writing this. I definitely wouldn't be doing this book. I wouldn't be sitting here in our office building with multiple businesses, preparing to speak, and thinking about my third book already. It wouldn't be possible if I let them decide my vision, but it's my choice. My success is up to me. Your success is up to you. If anyone can do it, we all can do it. You just got to see it. So look and find it, and have your vision. It's all yours. Be the architect of your life.

Chapter 11

Serenity

"Serenity is the tranquil balance of heart and mind." – Harold W. Becker

"Serenity is not freedom from the storm, but peace amid the storm."
– Unknown

This might be the toughest chapter to really do. The toughest one to go through is a struggle. We all know that. Those moments when we're down and out, they're the hardest; they're the hardest on us, but the hardest for us to do. This chapter really comes to mind. First, when I think of serenity, I think of acceptance. How many of us really accept where we are right now? How many of us accept that our relationships are the way they are right now, or that our businesses, our careers, or our professions are going in the way it's going right now? How many of us accept that our spiritual state, that our emotional state, or that our mental state is where it is right now? How many of us accept how our relationships are right now, not only with significant others, but also with our friends, our children, or our family? I am dragging this out already, but I am talking about any relationship that impacts your life.

How many of us are really accepting where we are? If we're not willing to accept where we are right now and if we're not willing to really look and say, "This is where I'm at," we never have the starting line to push towards the finish line no matter how cliche and cheesy it sounds. You cannot connect the dots correctly if you do not have the exact starting line and the finish line set when forging your path. The goal should always be what gives me the best chance to be the best me living the best life possible. Lying to yourself is NOT it!

"Many never get started." That's a quote used frequently. What they don't tell you is why people don't get started. We use terms like, "Oh, they procrastinate. Oh, they're lazy. Oh, they're just not dedicated. They really don't want it." I'm not such a believer in that. I believe everybody wants it. I've told individual clients and teams I've coached for over a decade, "Everybody wants to win. Everybody wants to be great. Everybody wants to be a millionaire." They might say they don't. They might say they don't care, but everybody wants it. They're not going to be like, "No, no, I don't want that." Everybody wants the great career, the great relationship, the great family, the great friends, or the great kids. Everybody. So to say they really don't want it, this is not true and a flat out lie. Everybody wants it.

There are two things that keep us from getting to the destination: not understanding and not being willing. I'm not willing to accept where I am. I have to accept where I am. I have to accept that right now, this is my position. This is my title. This is my family. These are the relationships I have with people, the close and the not so close ones. This is my career. This is the amount I make. This is the car I drive, and this is the house I live in. This is my life and all that encompasses it. Not only do you have to accept that, but you have to embrace it. You have to be brutally honest and have to be brutally honest with yourself about where you are in every aspect and accept it. Take it all in. It might not be all your fault. It might not be because of your hand. It might not be because of your reasoning, but you are where you are. Where you go from there is your responsibility and only yours.

Are you willing to accept that? If you're not, close this book. There's no point. Now, I'm not saying that's where you have to stay. Not at all. Heck, I'm begging you not to stay there, but that is where you are; there's no wrong spot to start. Starting where you are is the best spot, the only spot. This isn't to belittle you. This isn't because of society's opinions of anything in your life. Society's opinions of your life means nothing unless you let them. This isn't to bring you down-acceptance. This is so I can get started-acceptance.

It's like weight loss. There's something so motivating about someone that's completely out of shape and worked their butt off to get back into shape. I mean work their tails off, sometimes literally. Not because, no offense to anyone that did it. It's not a judgment, but they didn't do it the surgery way. They didn't do a quick fix and hope that it stays. They did a bust your ass every day, change your life, make decisions, make choices all the time, repeatedly, over and over again, to drop pounds to change their life.

There used to be a show, and this guy would come into one's life. He was a fitness guru, and he'd work with these people that were out of shape. I used to love this show. It was so motivating. They would get up early, and they would work out. They would do cardio.

They would eat better, and they would make better choices. They would drink more water. They'd start working out twice a day, and all of a sudden, in one year, the transformation was unbelievable. It made you know that if you dedicate yourself and put your mind to something, you're going to do it. It wasn't some legend. It wasn't some name bigger than life itself. It was everyday people living everyday life in everyday towns. It was nothing that you could try to proclaim to me with some kind of special path that they had like we try to do with people that make it big. There is no special DNA. Actually, that's wrong. Every DNA is special and capable of great things.

The best part of the show came after all that. They were so great at staying dedicated to the goal, and they did it so well that at the end, they would be available for the surgery to take away the excess skin from the amount of weight they lost. Really, sometimes I just go and Google that show because it empowers everyone because if anyone can, everyone can. It is amazing to see the realness of this show and the people in it.

One of the things they first do in that show, "What's your goal weight?" Nice. That's the goal. Where are you now? Get on the scale. And as painful as that moment is, and believe me, for them, it is painful, it is one of the most hurtful and toughest moments some go through. I've known people that are going through this and went through this, the process of trying to become healthier by losing weight, and that scale is a painful reminder. It's not pain because of failure. It's pain because it tells you exactly where you are. There's no fudging it, and there's no lying. There's no fake. That is what it is at that moment, and they have to accept it and that's tough.

It's tough to say, "Listen, my relationship isn't where I want it to be." It's tough to say, "My business isn't where I want it to be." It's tough to say, "My career is not where I want it to be." That's not easy. That's a hard answer because a lot of people will give you the cupcake. "Everything's amazing. Everything's great."

No, job's perfect. Family? Great. Right? How many people do you know at your office that you have daily conversations with? They all say the same answers to you. "Oh, everything's good," and now I wouldn't even want that dream job. They couldn't or wouldn't face anything going on in their life. They are only willing to tell everyone how great everything is even if it isn't true. It's never true. The issue isn't if you believe them or not. The problem is they believe themselves. I bet we all have ignored issues or lied to ourselves so much that we ended up believing it. The problem there is that leaves us at a delusional point in the journey that we have not yet achieved. We are not looking at the journey in the correct position. This makes it difficult or damn near impossible to move forward, hence that "I'm stuck" feeling you get at times. We do not want that because that delays the living part of life.

So I want you to take a break for a second. I want you to really write down where everything is in your life exactly where it is. Write down the job you work or the profession you have and the amount you make hourly or yearly. Write down the career you chose, or the job in which you chose that doesn't match up with the career you want, your friendships, and your relationships. List if you have any children or your family. Where are you mentally? Where are you personally? Where are you emotionally? Where are you physically? Write down your physical condition. Where are you? Take time and put down everything exactly where you are. Be brutally honest with yourself. If you are doing this right, it will be tough and might move you to tears, and that is OK. It is all part of living your best life as the best version of yourself. Please do not take the easy way out. No pain, no gain. Be willing to be real with yourself. Take some time. I'm proud of you for being willing.

Listen, there are no wrong answers here if you were honest. This isn't right or wrong. This is the starting line. We needed to know where it is before we can say go, but we need to be able to say go to get to the finish line. So as painful as this exercise could be or was, you have to do it, and you have to be honest. Checking yourself is one of three musts to achieving the best you. You have to be very honest with yourself, and don't think of this as punishment. This isn't bad.

This is saying you are dedicated to growing as you. Don't be mad at yourself for your answers. Be motivated because this is where you're going to come out of. This is what your story is going to say. This is, at the end, you could tell your friends, your family, your relationships, and your kids, "This is where I started and look where I ended." No excuses, none for you, and you're going to motivate people around you. You might not be able to see it, but you'll do it. They might not let you know it, but you did it. Earlier I said I am proud of you, but I am hoping you are proud of yourself because that is much more important.

You know what that takes? The next part of this serenity is courage. It takes courage to be able to say, "I'm not where I want to be." It takes courage to be able to say, "This is where I am now." It takes courage to take on challenges. It takes courage to look adversity in the eyes and to look up the mountain top but see the mountain and start climbing anyway. It takes courage to do that. I do not want you to think I am making anything about this process easy. It isn't. John Maxwell said, "Everything worth having is up hill," and you will hear me say it often. We call them mountains for a reason: it is hard and takes time to conquer them.

It is no surprise people every day try to pawn that off. People every day try not to look like they are climbing but already there. People every day try to look like they're already on top of the mountain when you know it's only because they have never climbed one. There are mountains of pebbles, and they're standing on it. I tell you, after you do this, you will get to your mountain top if you keep going. If you do this and you stay dedicated to it and you know you want to unleash your greatness on whatever it is you're doing, when you get to your mountain top and you will, you will find another mountain to climb. After you do it, Oh, the rush, man. Oh, the feeling of a utopia runs through you, one of confidence and belief. You will change and it will be an amazing change. You embrace yourself. Hell, you seek it.

How many of us are willing to embrace ourselves? I don't mean hug yourself in a corner. How many of you embrace who you truly are for all the things that society might say is a flaw, for all the failures in which you went through, and for all the scars in which you earned inside and out. That takes courage. That's tough. Accepting truth about yourself and accepting the challenge to get to where you want to be is a treacherous road, all uphill, and takes extreme courage. The good news is, we are all capable of performing this act. We all can do it. It's up to each of us.

Believe me, what I'm telling you about is a journey. I've been going down (really up) this road for years, and it isn't easy. Sometimes it's still not easy, and I still have those moments of self-doubt. I question if it's all worth it. Is it worth the pain? It is. Sometimes it is painful, and this isn't a one time thing. I wish it was, but you're going to have to check yourself quite a bit. That's the only way you can make your starting line and keep advancing it. You have to be willing to accept it. You have to be willing to embrace it. You have to be willing to have the courage to go from it. You have to take it all in and get moving. This whole thing is about embracing yourself: embracing where you are, embracing where you want to go, and embracing how it is going to be to get there. Know it's going to take an awful lot of courage, and along the way, the next part of this is learning from it all. You're going to need to gain wisdom from your journey from both the good and the bad parts.

Listen, gain the wisdom that you don't like it where you are. You don't like this feeling. You don't like this starting line. You're not supposed to like the starting line. You're supposed to love the finish line. It has to make you mad. It has to make your blood boil that you're not where you want to be, and you have to learn every little thing you can from it. You have to learn from people around you. Read books and learn from books as much as you can. There's knowledge everywhere. There's knowledge from people in the field in which you want to go into. No, I'm not saying do everything they say to do, but you can get knowledge from their stories. We all have stories. We can gain understanding. We can gain knowledge and information. What we call that altogether is wisdom. Learn the things you like and align with you but also learn the things that you want to stay away from. Learn what to do and what not to do. Learning doesn't mean agreeing or copying. I bet you learned from a parent or guardian things you like and want to do as one and things you do not want to do as one. That's all I am trying to tell you.

You need the wisdom. Some people only learn by doing. Some people can learn by others' mistakes. When they were trying to create flight, people were jumping off platforms with fake wings. Do you think the next guy that was coming along to create flight was like, "Man, I need to jump off a platform with wings on too because that guy did it?" Or he was like, "All right, that doesn't work. We need to do something different." You can learn from other people even if it's not what to do. It might be what not to do, but you need to gain the wisdom and understanding along the way. You need to be willing to take in information. You need to be willing to adjust your approach. Gain knowledge and apply it to your life; this will create the quickest growth and save you valuable time along your journey.

I always think people get confused when I bring this up because of my "You always have to be you message." I have to be me that part is all true. Yes. That doesn't mean you have to do the same thing over and over again. You do not have to make the same mistake another person did just so you can say you did it to. You can gain it from others as well. Your attitude is so important to how others will help you along the way. Also, when it comes to attitude, that doesn't mean you have to have the same attitude all the time because then I don't feel like that's you. I feel like that's an act. No one has the same attitude all the time. If you act like you do, that's exactly what it is, an act. You are human, so you will not always be happy, glad, sad, mad, or any other way here. It's good to go through the cycle of being yourself and embrace all of you, not just the good or the bad or the proud or embarrassed.

We need to be able to learn. If you want to create influence, you need to learn how to influence people. If you want to lead, you have to learn how to lead people. If you want to be the best marketer, you have to learn how to market. That's another thing about learning people. Listen, almost any field, career, position, relationship, or anything you want to do is going to involve people.

A story about me: when I first started coaching … It might not be that great of a story actually, but when I first started coaching, I said, "Oh, I don't want to do anything with relationships."

One of the instructors looked at me and laughed and was like, "What kind of coaching are you going to do if you don't do anything with relationships?"

I was like, "Oh, I don't know, maybe a success coach, a transformational coach."

They were like, "Well, you know, they normally have to deal with transformational coach relationships, success coach relationships, any kind of coach relationships, any kind of work relationships, and of course the obvious, any kind of relationship relationships, but almost everything that has to do with coaching involves working with other people. That is relationships, and you have to be willing to learn how to do it."

How do people tick? How do you tick? You have to gain wisdom from other people, from books, from movies, from motivational quotes, from inspirational videos, from YouTube, from podcasts, from daily conversations, and from random conversations. Seek them out. Seek out gaining wisdom and also from your own experiences. I use this example a lot. There's a hot stove and you touch it. It burns you. You learned don't touch the stove. Make sure it's not on or hot first. You don't just keep touching the stove. You know why? You learned. You have grown and even if painful, it is good to grow.

My dad was the best at letting me learn through my actions. As much now as I wish he didn't, it's true nonetheless. We used to have this flimsy TV stand. I have no idea why we had it. It was like fake gold and V'd in, and there was just this little pipe in the middle and then this platform on top. Clearly, by anyone's means, this was not a good TV stand. I don't even know if that's what it was really made for because how badly it was made if it was for that. That's what my dad put a TV on, and he did not care what I thought.

I used to go underneath it and play with the stand because it was great for matchbox cars, and my mom would always say, "Look out. Don't play underneath there. Don't play underneath there. Don't play underneath there." It was the only place where I had the really cool ramp, also known as the TV stand, so I kept doing it. My dad would always say, "Give it time, he'll learn. Give it time, he'll learn," and I had no idea what he was talking about. Then one day I hit the TV stand too hard, and the TV fell on me. And it hurt. It hurt bad. I don't understand why my dad let that happen, like this could have been serious injuries, but you know what? I never played on that ramp again. I never used that as my ramp. I figured another way because I learned. I learned so well I never touched anything near that TV stand for the rest of the time we had it. It was a hell of a learning situation…

The part isn't where the TV fell on me that made me learn, the part is way before that moment I could have learned from my mom telling me. When are you going to take the wisdom being shared to you? Will you take it from books, other people's stories, or wherever you find the message whether audio or visual, or are you going to have to make the mistake yourself? I'll tell you this: the quicker you learn, the quicker you'll advance. I wish I learned from my mom's words instead of the pain of the TV falling on my legs. I had the chance but I was too stubborn and just not smart enough to take the words as a lesson before the pain part of it.

This is very easy. Right now, we're going step by step on how to do this. The chapter is called "Serenity." It should be called "X Marks the Spot." We're telling that this … you have to accept where you are, your starting point, and the courage to go. That's where you're starting to go forward towards your goal, towards the top of the mountain, and the wisdom to learn to be able to get up there faster.

Next, what else do you need? Faith. I'm not saying God or whatever you call it; I'm saying faith in you that you'll make it, that you won't stop until you do, that you'll figure it out, and that you'll get there. Have faith you were made for something bigger than whatever it is you're doing, and I don't care how big of what you're doing is now. Have faith that you can do something bigger, you can do something great, or you could make a greater impact. You can change lives, no matter if you change more of them or one of them. Have faith in yourself and all you want to accomplish in this life.

I should never have more faith in you than you do, and right now I'm telling you, you have greatness within you waiting just to be tapped into. It is waiting for you to perfect it, waiting for you to hone it, and waiting for you to find what you believe is your calling, your passion, and your purpose and what you are doing here. Unleash your greatness on all of us. Go all out on it and give it everything you've have. It's waiting for you. Heck, it's begging you to let it out. Your greatness is whispering to you. It's screaming inside you. When are you going to have the faith to believe it and listen to it? Because when you do and when you keep it, your life changes. The game changes. Your vision will change. Your feelings will change. You'll smile brighter. You'll be down less. You'll be up more because you know the mission. You know the cause. You know what you're going after. You see it, you feel it, and you believe in it. You aren't talking about happy or sad anymore but fulfillment because no matter the type of day, when you have fulfillment everything is better.

When you align yourself with this, everything's different. The bad's not as bad; we know we're going to go through struggles. We know we're going to have trials and tribulations. We know we're going to have bad times and hard times, but it's so much better when we see what we're going after and what we're willing to fight for. So, stop just going through the motions. Stop just being willing to accept the bad and start forgoing the good. Start bringing the great. Unleash your greatness and leave your impact: the kind of impact that will be felt for a long, long time, if not forever. Be willing to do it. Be willing to believe in it.

I don't think this is what I'm here for. I know this is what I'm here for. I believe it wholeheartedly. I'm here to impact lives. I'm here to make people see their greatness and know they aren't alone. I am here to show people that we are all significant. I'm here for them to live their best life as the best version of themselves. That's what I'm here to do. When I started off, I had a little niche. I was a basketball coach. That was my niche. I knew the game of basketball, and I could impact lives. That was my niche. It was a very little niche, but through that, I have impacted thousands of young men and women.

Then I grew. I was an entrepreneur's coach because I started my own businesses, and I had my own businesses. I had another little niche. They kept telling me, "Have your niche. Master it, master it, master it."

Then I said, "You know what? I can change lives. I can impact people. I can help people because that's what I want to do. That's what I'm motivated to do. That's what I'm focused on doing. That's what I have faith in doing. That's what I've been learning about. That's what I have the courage to chase."

So, I'm not going to little niche myself. Whatever your issue is, I'm here to help. Whatever you want to accomplish, I'm here to help. I'm the you-can-do-it coach. It's funny because I normally say it in that accent. You can do it. That's not a little niche. You want to do something? I'm here. Let's go. Let's make it happen. That's what makes me excited. I became a high performance success coach, and we will get you to where you want to be.

The next part and the final part of this chapter is to keep moving forward. Now, you're going to get hit. You're going to hit with stumbling blocks, you're going to hit roadblocks, you're going to hit cement walls, and you're going to hit barriers. Be water. Go around it, go through it, go over it, and go underneath it. If you keep moving forward, you will wear that barrier down. Keep moving forward. Take a rest, fall down, and take a break or whatever you want to call it but keep moving forward daily. Another John Maxwell quote, "You don't have to to do it all day, but you should do it everyday." He is so right. Move forward daily. Get closer daily. Move on the path daily.

When I was thinking about this chapter and was thinking about serenity and all the things we've talked about, an actor, who I've always been like up and down on in my life, came up. I have to say a little bit about him. Keanu Reeves is the actor in which I'm talking about. You know when he was 3 years old, his father abandoned him? He didn't see his dad again for like 10 years, till he was 13 or more years old. He moved around a lot making it hard to gain friendships. His mom was married and divorced 4 times. He went to a handful of high schools in a 5-year period, and then he dropped out and just moved to Los Angeles.

One of his stepfathers was a Hollywood actor, and that's how he gained his green card. In 1998, he got married and had a baby, who was eventually born still born at 8 months, which tore down and destroyed the relationship. After only 18 months after the relationship ended, his wife, ex-wife, died in a car accident. He just kept believing. He just kept pushing forward. I cannot even begin to imagine how hard each of these moments were for him. The strength it took to keep going has to be the strongest substance on earth ... Heart.

Any of these could have been a good enough reason for him to stop, and any of these could have broke him and is understandable. He's one of the most inspirational and uplifting men you will hear. If you ever get a chance, listen to some of his speeches and quotes. He's so down to earth. He's so generous when he's went through so many failures. You could have said this guy was destroyed from birth or from 3 years old. His dad left me, and he didn't see him for a decade or more. He went through numerous different relationships. He watched his mom get divorced multiple times. He went to multiple high schools in a 5- year period, and he eventually became a high school dropout. He had a stillborn baby and the woman he loved and married died. Any of these moments could have broken him, left him broken, or let him quit because he was broken. There were so many reasons to not start again or to not risk that hurt again but still.

What happened? The more he broke, the more light shined through. He was always honest about where he was. He accepted the line in which he was at, the starting point. He had the courage to keep going. He learned along the way. If you listen to some of his quotes and videos, I promise you, you'll see. He had faith and he kept moving forward. Wow. The strength it takes I can only imagine.

Now, you probably haven't been through those things, but you still have been through things. It's going to take strength and courage to keep going. Do not down play your trial and tribulations because they aren't his. We all handle things differently and are all impacted differently. So embrace it, learn from it, and keep going What's the alternative? Just sit in the pain? Well, that would be one hell of a bad acceptance. Don't accept that. Accept where you are as your starting line and get going. I believe in you. It's time for you to believe in yourself. You have some mountains to climb!

Chapter 12

TIMMY SAID IT: "BE HUMBLE AND KIND."

"I am humble enough to know I am not better than anyone else, but wise enough to know I am different."
– Unknown

"True humility is not thinking less of yourself; it is thinking of yourself less."
– Rick Warren

It's one of my favorite songs not because it's by Tim McGraw. He's cool, but just the message in the song needs to be heard and remembered often. I have it on pretty much every playlist I created on my iTunes. I think we all need this reminder here and there, but I know I do. It is so easy to be kind but so often we choose not to be.

I used to get so worked up when someone was rude to me, but I figured the reason. There is this quote that goes around about people that treat you poorly do so because what they are going through and feeling. No, that does not make it better or right, but it did change the way I looked at it. That made me aware that it wasn't about me at all, it was about them. They are going through something, and when I thought that, it made me feel bad for them. Crazy right?!?!? It isn't all about me.

I don't know if you know how important this part of it is, to be able to fully gain everything we want in life. Being humble and kind play a huge role in everything we want in our relationships, everything we want in our family, everything we want in our marriage, everything we want in our friendships, everything we want in our career, in our profession, and in our calling, everything we want spiritually, everything we want mentally or emotionally, even financially. If you don't know what a big part being humble and kind play in it, you're going to fall short. Also, it will probably make you miserable, and no one really wants to be that.

I remember this phrase I once heard, and I love it. It said, "Your attitude will normally determine your altitude." How high will you get normally comes down to how you act and how you treat people. I have worked with people that were less qualified that had amazing attitudes, that were so kind and generous, that had big old loving hearts, and that were humble. They gave so much, and some of them still do. It inspires me to do more and to give more. It also made me want to work with those people and give more opportunities to those people. The person being a big old jerk is not going to make me want to give more chances or opportunities to. I am sure we all know some people that would be so much further in life if they were just kinder or nicer to others. It is simple but sometimes we forget the simple things.

The be humble part is not wanting to brag, not wanting to rub what you do in everybody's face. Or not wanting to be the talk of the town. Listen, if you are, you will be. You do not have to tell everyone. You don't have to do it for them. Amazing as you are, you don't have to tell everybody. You can just appreciate that they notice your greatness. I believe this whole wholeheartedly. If you are good at something, people will notice. If you have to tell them you are, well, you probably aren't as good as you think. Sorry but it is sooo true!

They did this study. It was about the best kind of leaders, and it came down that this combination was called "humbly narcissistic." Narcissistic means a "strong belief in self." Humble means that you know you're fallible. It means that you know you'll make mistakes and that you're human. That makes you like everyone else, because remember, as far as you climb, the people you pass along the way will be the ones holding you up. I don't know how much they'll want to hold you up if you're not being very cool with them and if you're a big old jerk, right? If your ego's out of this world, no one will be willing to help or hold your weight.

I'm not saying act like you don't know what you've done. I'm not saying in certain conversations when things are talked about to speak your knowledge and to speak your truth. I'm not telling you not to do that. You can still be able to do that while still being humble, while still knowing your position and your part and what it does for everyone else. You can do that without trying to put others lower or down. You should be able to be you without making others feel less. Heck, the best do it while making the others feel greater.

Remember, you made mistakes. Remember, the wrong you've done. You failed. You were down and out. You did bad deeds. Now you fought through them. You either kept going until you made it, or you're still going through it and still fighting 'til you make it. You will have battles just like you already had battles no matter if you go for your greatness or not. If we know that to be true, there is no point in not trying for the best you living your best life possible. Be committed to getting to the best parts no matter how hard the rough times hit you.

Now, understand that some people might be behind you in this journey. They might not have gotten to where you've gotten to yet in their path and their journey because there's no time table on this. There's no expiration date. There's only one, and that's when we take the last breath. Just because they might not be where you are along the journey, that doesn't mean they won't get there or won't get even further, so be humble with it. Be humble about it. Be willing not to have to be in the spotlight. Even more importantly, when you are in that light, you do not have to rub it in that you are there. Some will let you know it. Some will be so happy for you, and others will hate on you for it. That is life and it will not change, but that doesn't mean you have to change either. You can lead by the example you set when you are low and when you are high. Listen, your haters will already be bothered by your success if you say it or not. So stay classy my friend and show them how winners act. The point you wanted was the goal, not talking to everyone about how you accomplished the goal. Some will ask because they want to make it as well, and that is fine to talk with them about your path. That is not the same thing as rubbing into their face. Even when others go low, you can be yourself. Be humble.

The other part is to be kind. We need to care about people more. Be kind to one another. Think about others. Think about how we can give back. Think about what you can do for others. I talked about it before in this book. One of the greatest things I love about the foundation I'm part of—named in honor of my brother—is that we try to do so much for so many and we love it. We think of ideas nonstop. We have people that give their time on holidays to be part of the things we're doing, trying to give back, trying to show love, trying to make sure people know they're not alone, that people care, and trying to give kindness and to spread it. If we understand the better others are doing, the better chance I have to do better. It might be a completely selfish way to look at it, but if that's what you need, I will give it to you. Helping others works both ways. They get some help out of it for sure, but you also get out of it to. First, the feeling you get when you give is something like a natural high. Also, the more they advance, it opens doors for you to advance as well. That is the ultimate win win.

I see people give up time with family, traditions on holidays, and so much more just to do it, just to be part of it, just to give back, and just to spread love and kindness. It inspires me. It motivates me. I want to do more. We do an event once a year and see how many people we serve. I want to do it more. I want to do it bigger. I want to impact more people. We go back to the drawing board and think of ways to do it better and bigger, not for the spotlight but for the ability to help more and more. The more we help, the more opportunity the people have including us. The more we help, the more opportunity the kids will have and the grandkids will have. We move the flag further down the field for this generation and all the next ones to come. The point of each and everyone of us is to make progress for all, especially the ones to come after. We all should of heard the phrase, "Leave it better than you found it." We can do that at the grandest scale; we can leave this world better than we found it.

I don't feel bad about it because of how good it makes me feel to do it. It is great to feel good for doing good for others. That isn't selfish or being a jerk. Feeling good for doing good on a test or a business deal is great, but nothing should compare to doing good for others. You can be kind every day. Are you willing to hold that door for the person behind you in the store? Are you willing to pick up something if someone drops it? Are you willing to grab someone's shopping cart so they don't have to walk and put it back? Are you willing to grab a shopping cart in a parking lot because someone was inconsiderate and just left it in the middle of a spot? Help someone carry something when they can't lift it? Are you willing to smile and say, "How are you?" or "Good morning!" "Good afternoon!" or "Goodnight!"? These are not big things but can mean something special to someone else. Remember we have no idea what battles they are facing, but we are all facing some. I bet you have days that you would love for someone to be kind for a second just to change your thinking or focus. Why not be that person to others? I remember growing up listening to the music group, Arrested Development. I loved their sound. They had a song named "Mister Wendal," and I still jam to that song this very day. Heck, I am going to turn it on now and you should too! But in that song they reference a line about how a little bit of money might not be a big deal to some, but it can mean a world of difference to another person. I think of that line often because something might be insignificant to you but to the other person might be exactly what they need to make it through this day. It doesn't have to be money like we talked about, sometimes a smile is all that is needed to lift someone up.

It's the little things, like those little acts of kindness that can change someone's day, can change someone's life, and can take them out of a dark place or a bad place, or even just enhance a good one. Those little things matter. Are you willing to be someone that will do those little things? Because they add up. Little things add up to the big things. I don't like when people talk about them like they're not one and the same. The big things and the little things are the same. The only difference is when you think about a big thing, it's multiple things part of it, or the moment is bigger. Little things, are just the big things broken down into pieces for us to see better. They are all the same and when put together weigh the same. If you don't have the little things, you can't have the big things. This book is about becoming the best you. It is about finding your success, and that's a big thing. So we break it down into chapters to see the little parts that add up. If we do some or most of these things, well, we will most likely get closer to where we want to go. Heck, we might get all the way there.

Your relationship, that's a big thing, how you communicate and how you're dedicated to it. Are you willing to learn the other person and what they need in the relationship? Are you willing to spend time, money, and effort to work through the bad and the fights that will come with any relationship in enough time? Those are all little things, but they're all the big thing. Those little things are all your relationship. We talked about them like they weren't the same, but they are one and the same. One's part of the other. So be kind. Be humble and care about one another. Life is a team sport; don't try to do it alone.

I used a key phrase earlier in this chapter. It's this word called "serve." I work with some business owners. I work with professionals. I work with athletes, CEOs, entrepreneurs, small business owners, and students. I work with many people in many different walks of life. But one thing is always true, and it's normally one of the first things I say to them. "Who do you serve? How do you serve them? How can you serve them better? How you can serve them more?" But more importantly, how can I serve you to make that possible? See, how that works is we all need to know who we serve, how we serve them, and how others can help us serve them even better. A life of meaning is a life of service-hood. We serve others daily from family, to friends, to coworkers, to the community, to customers, and even strangers.

It's a simple thing. When anybody asks me any question like this, "What can I do to get this job?" or "What can I do to get the business I want?" or "What can I do to get the playing time I want?" or "What can I do to get into the career field I want?"

I say this: "Serve. Serve more. Serve greater. Be eager to serve." If you aren't about serving others, there is not much hope for you or your business with me. I most likely can not help you much. If it's all about you, we probably will not make it far together.

I went to the John Maxwell Conference in Orlando. It was amazing. If you ever get to or think about it, you should check it out. He told a story about his grandson when he went to work, and his grandson said, "How can I work my way up and be an asset to the company and get to where I want to get to?" He said, "Go in early. Be set up, ready, and working before the time you're supposed to be there. Instead at lunch if you get an hour, take a half hour. Work for 30 minutes. Stay late sometimes. Get things done. Get projects done. Go into your boss' office and ask, 'What else can I do for you? Is there anything you need help with or are there projects that you could use an extra hand with?' Do those things. You'll be a hit. You'll move farther than everybody else that comes around the same time. Why? All those things come down to serving. Be willing to serve. Be willing to serve more. Be willing to serve longer." Be willing to sacrifice. It all comes down to what are you willing to give.

I coach basketball; I absolutely love it. Coaching sports, coaching the game of basketball is my first line of coaching. I coach at a local college, and it's awesome. The whole time I'm asking these guys, "How can I better serve you? Where do you need me to serve you? Because it's not just where I want to serve you. It can't be just Xs and Os. It can't just be having fun at practice, just basketball information, or fundamentals of the game, right? How can I serve you better than just that?"

They started opening up to me. They said, "Coach, we could use better meal ideas during the winter break." So, I worked to serve them better for meals during winter break. They said, "Coach, we could use some opportunities to be able to get into different lines of work during our off time to be able to earn a little money." So, we set up a resume, their interviewing skills, and set them up to get interviews with different businesses to improve their skills to get the jobs they seek. They learn skills now and build connections for the future.

Better serving. How do you better serve the people around you? How can you better serve the people you work with? How can you better serve your family, your friends, your coworkers, your boss, or your clients? On and on. How can you better serve your neighborhood or your community? Because I'll tell you this. The better you serve, the more you get. Let me say that again so you don't miss it. The better you serve, the more you'll get. I said it earlier, and Ill keep saying it. Life of service.

Now, let me tell you, I've been there. Believe me. I've been in situations where I gave a lot. I served and they did nothing for me. They didn't serve back, and you don't do it thinking they're going to serve back. You do it because that's who you are, and this is what's going happen. They might not notice. They might not appreciate. They might not be willing to give you the due you've earned by how in service you are, but someone's going to. People outside and people from other companies or rivals will notice. Of course, coaching basketball for as long as I have, other schools and coaches come up and ask me if I ever think of leaving and would love to have me. People will notice when you are putting it in. It might not be the one you were hoping for, but it might be the right one. The one you need to keep growing to become closer to the best you. People will notice!

I've had coaches say they love the passion I have. I've had coaches come and talk to me about the relationship I have with players, and sometimes the coaches I've coached with haven't told me these things. Just because you think this person's supposed to notice or this company's supposed to notice, they might not, but someone's going to. You serve hard enough long enough, someone's going to notice it. It might not be the ones that were supposed to appreciate it but someone will. People miss what they have, but others that do not have will want it. You do it because who you are not because who they are.

That will get you more opportunities because the kind of person you are and because the kind of leader you are is the one that's going to serve first and serve often. You will serve when you might not get anything back, and that can be just all right because the satisfaction, that feeling you get, it's a natural drug. I'm addicted to that feeling of giving and of serving. I seek it.

Now, listen. Sometimes those you serve will not get it. Sometimes the response isn't what we envisioned getting. Sometimes the person chose not yet to be at that point in the journey at which you are. We have to understand, it's not for them to understand, for them to get it, or for them to be appreciative of what you do. So then add value back or work to expand the way you add value or your position in which you can add value in. You do not do this for the spotlight, you do this because that's who you are. No matter if they notice or not because at some point, they will notice either when you are there or when you left because someone else noticed. I go to stores and restaurants and when I notice a hard worker going above and beyond, I will drop my card with them. I tell them I notice how hard they are working and serving others, and we could always use that at the companies I am part of. No, they do not always call but at least they know someone notices.

I always want the people highest with me that serve. If you're willing to serve early and often, I want you around because the more people doing that, the more likely we will actually achieve our goals and get where we want to get to. The best life is a real option when multiple people are working together to achieve it. That means it's not just on one of us to push all the weight. If I am tired, they can help me and vice versa.

There's a metaphor that was used once. It's everything you retain is in this cup. Let's say it's one of those red Solo cups. We should all know red Solo cups. Everything you retain is in there, and it keeps filling and filling and filling up until it's to the brim. Now it can just overflow if you want, or you can pour some into other people's cups so now they get some too. That opens room for you to get more. It shows how giving also opens up for receiving.

You see what I mean there? If my cup is full, I can't take anymore in. I have to be willing and able and understand, I need to pour some out to other people, to people in my community, people in my family, my loved ones, my friends, people in my business, and my coworkers and on and on.

Whatever it is, whoever it is, or wherever it is, you have to be willing to pour some of your cup out. You have to be willing to give what's in your cup, so you can receive more and receive differently. You have to be willing to share what's in your cup, so you can move onto the next step, next stage, or next level because if you don't, if you just try to hold all your cup, you're just going to lose some of it and never gain more. You will be stuck, and being stuck means, you are falling behind.

So be willing to give your cup because at the end of the day, this isn't about you. This is greater than you. The cause is greater than us all. That's one of the first things I always say when people come into the foundation's office. I'll tell them, "The cause is bigger than us," but if God calls my number tomorrow, the foundation is going to open; they're going continue with the mission even if I'm not there. That's how strong it is. That's how big it is. The meaning and passion behind it is bigger than any one person.

I once heard, "If you want to see how small you really are, look up to the stars." I want to tell you if you want to know how small you are, look at the things that are happening around you. I hope they're so big that you go, "Man, I might just have a little piece in this, but I have a piece. And it's part of something so much bigger." Our gift is meant to be given away. Our gift is meant to be experienced by the world. Our art is meant to be enjoyed by others. Our life is meant to be felt by others. Robin Williams says that line they use in commercials now where Whitman wrote "That the powerful play goes on, and you may to contribute a verse". Really think about that. Are you contributing a verse? What is your verse saying? What will your verse be?

This is so much bigger than just self. It's bigger than just me, or I, or even the team I have. This is bigger than just a personal goal and a personal objective. This is bigger than us. Be part of something bigger than you. To be part of something greater than one individual is the best way to go through this game of life. Be greater than any one individual could ever be.

When I was doing this chapter, I figured out who I was going to use pretty early in the process. You might recognize the last name. The first name, not so much. Soichiro, last name, Honda. I'm sure you know, a Japanese inventor, the automotive empire you know by his name, Honda. But it didn't start that way. At 15, he really didn't have a formal education. As a teenager he left his home and went to Tokyo looking for work. He got an auto repair shop job. He was there for six years before going back home to open up his own shop.

During the Great Depression at the age of 31, he founded his own store and his own shop to create piston rings for Toyota. He labored all day long to make these parts. He had very little cash left and very little chances left for survival, especially in that field. He had to pawn his wife's ring and even though he did all that, he still failed. They said his rings weren't good enough, and they weren't going work. But he wouldn't give up. He ended up going back to school, always searching for ways to improve himself and his designs. He was going to grow to the point where he could make the right part the best way.

Two years after that, he finally succeeded and secured a contract with Toyota. But right after that happened, the factory that he just built was hit by a bomb during World War II. Then, he rebuilt the factory another time and an earthquake leveled it. But he still would not quit. He would then go on to create a motorized bike known as the motorcycle and started Honda Motorcycles.

He had many times when he could have quit and many times when he could have given up. He could have changed his whole mindset, his whole attitude, and his whole belief, and he didn't. Even after all those failures, he was known as one of the kind-hearted people on Earth. He gave back and gave opportunities to people in his community. Even during the tough times when money was tight, he kept a positive mindset, a kind demeanor, and a kind heart. We can all learn something from him, from Mr. Honda. We can all get something from it.

He stayed humble, and he stayed kind. He didn't quit. He gave to others and stayed true to who he was. He left an impact bigger than himself that continues to this very day. We all know Honda, but now you know the man behind it.

If you have a chance today, listen to Tim McGraw's song, "Humble and Kind," and remember throughout your journey, being humble and kind can be one of your greatest assets. How high are you willing to fly because your attitude determines your altitude? How much are you willing to give? How much are you willing to serve? Not just when it's convenient, not just when it's your way, when it's the way that's needed, or when it's someone else's way. Are you still going to be willing to serve? Are you smiling, or are you frowning? Are you celebrating for your people's wins, or are you trying to cool-guy it?

I know it's hard, believe me. I know it's hard, and I know people will give you many reasons not to be this way. Believe me. I lent money to people that never planned to pay me back. I've bought houses, cars, and paid bills for people that wouldn't even buy my book. I've supported multiple people's events or businesses that never supported mine. But you can't let it change who you are because who you are is greater than the actions of others.

I've then seen people give up holidays to serve people food. They give up paychecks to make sure others around them are rewarded for their work and their effort. They gave up Christmas gifts so others would get some. They gave up time to give it to others. You choose what you see and look at. Choose to be part of the good, and to do that, you have to be willing to see the good and not just focus on the things that you don't like, the things that upset you, or things you don't feel are fair. Don't let the way someone else lives their life affect yours. So no matter what's happening around you, listen to Timmy. Be humble and kind. Your success will be determined by what value you add. The more value you add, the better chance you have. So what are you doing to add value? What can you do to add more of it? How are you serving others? How can you serve more? Now that you know, go do it.

Chapter 13

Your Masterpiece

"Everyday you are adding to your masterpiece, make sure its something that they will want to look at for all time." – Michael Fabber

We all have seen the Sistine Chapel, the Mona Lisa, Michelangelo's David, and the Statue of Liberty or any other piece of artwork that's been cherished, loved, and known for years to most of us. But everyone doesn't know we all have that masterpiece waiting to be created, and it's in every single one of us. No, I'm not just blowing smoke up your ass. No, I'm not telling you it's going to be easy. No, I'm not telling you we're all painters or sculptors. What I'm telling you is what I've been telling you this whole time, and if you made it this far, you should know it already. It is that you and everyone around you has greatness within them, and with that greatness, we are going to create a masterpiece. That masterpiece is going to be whatever your passion is, your purpose is, and your calling is. I don't care if it's the greatest basketball player or team ever assembled. I don't care if it's the greatest entrée ever created. I don't care if it's the cleanest sidewalks, streets, or hallways in your community. Whatever it is, it's your masterpiece. There is no bad masterpiece. No one ever said, "Man, look at that masterpiece. It's horrible." And they won't with you. You won't be the first to have a bad masterpiece. Also, forget the judgement of others and the terms "good" or "bad." It isn't about them. This is all about you living your best life as the best you. You doing your thing and creating your masterpiece at worst gives others the power to do theirs. This moves the flag further for the next generation to take it and move it even farther. But if we do not, then we didn't do our part, and worse, we didn't have the life we could have, heck, should have had. So do your thing and make your masterpiece.

But in order to have your masterpiece, you have to be willing to go for it. You have to know you're going to have hard times. You're going to have setbacks, and you're going to have failures along the way. It's going to be tough but life is at times. It's going to take time, but all great things do. It's going to be a pain in the ass, but so are most of the greatest things that happen. The journey has rough parts, but at least these rough parts are worth it for the reward of you living your best life. My daughter keeps telling me I am saying that phrase too much, but there is a reason. I need you to accept the fact you aren't living that life, but also know you can if you are just willing to go for it. Believe me, I was the guy that was willing to cool-guy my life away. I was great at just doing enough. I played it safer than most and did it well. While I was doing that, I was getting dragged through all kinds of painful situations: I was losing people I loved, was failing at endeavors, and was struggling to figure out how to make ends meet without having my handout hoping someone would help. That's when it hit me, I was playing it super safe and still had to deal with all this crap. If I had to deal with it either way, I might as well go for the life I want and the life that I am meant to live. I might as well go to be great and be the best me possible doing great things by creating great impact. So, now let me turn it to you. Are you going through or have gone through some shit? Have you experienced pain? Have you had your ass kicked? Have you failed? Have you felt disappointment? If you are being honest, the answer is yes, so why not go for it? If you already get the crap part, you might as well get the amazing part as well. Do not just survive this trip my friend. They say life hits you hard, but are you going to hit back?

Also, I don't just mean in your work, your masterpiece is so much more than your career. It's all aspects of your life: your family, your friends, your relationships, your career or profession, your emotional state, your spiritual state, and your mental state. Combine it all and make your masterpiece with the impact in which you leave on others and the gifts you leave for others. I'm not talking about material things only. This is all part of your masterpiece. Your masterpiece can be the combination of all the areas of your life, and that's why I want you to make time for them all. Make time for your mental state because your inner peace is key. Make time for your emotional state and spiritual state and all the relationships you have, and what you leave in their heart will come together and create your masterpiece. How do you want it to look? How do you want it to be seen and remembered? The great part is it is all up to you. No one else controls this, but that also means there are no excuses.

I pray you never get to see it. Think about the greatest artists. Most of them didn't get to see the appreciation for their art or what it is now. Think about some of the greatest composers that never got to see how we appreciated what they did. Think of the greatest poets and writers. Most of them didn't get to see how much we cherish their work and their words. Many masterpieces have never even been witnessed by the ones that created it because their masterpiece wasn't for them. Their masterpiece was for the rest of us, to give us hope, to give us belief, and to give us whatever feeling it creates within us: to be willing to keep going, to not feel alone, to feel connected to something, and to feel peace in something, and that's just one aspect of their masterpiece. It was for us to be inspired and restored belief.

Your masterpiece can do that as well, whatever it is. There is no right or wrong masterpiece. It's just your masterpiece, but you have to create it because if you don't, no one will for you. If you don't, no one will ever know the verse in which you contributed to this world and to this life. You're going to say, "How can I create something that will impact as many as the Sistine Chapel has?" How do you know it won't? How do you know it won't reach the masses? How do you know it won't impact miles and miles wide?

But more importantly, what if you're only meant to impact one that way? Is that any less important? Is that any less of a task to create a masterpiece that moves one to change the world? One can be moved to create a movement simply by the impact that you left them and maybe just them. There is no predetermined total that will make your impact worthy or not. The ripple effect might just need to hit the right one that will carry it further, or it will hit hundreds to carry it further. But the point is for it to be carried further. For that to happen, you have to do your part first. You have to paint your masterpiece. The biggest of fires are created by a single spark.

Most people know of Tony Robbins. Less people know of Jim Rohn. Jim Rohn was Tony Robbin's mentor. If all Jim Rohn did was impact Tony Robbins, even though he didn't, but if that's all he did, his impact on Tony has created impact on masses. That's how important your masterpiece is. There is no set path, and there is no set way to create yours. You have to figure it out and decide how will yours look to the rest of us. You're going to do it by trial and error. You're going to do it by practice. You're going to do it by learning from failure. You're going to do it by adjusting plans, creating different ways, going for different things, and embracing different ideas. That's how you do it, and it's going to take time. Lots of time. God willing, we all have it, but no matter when you leave this place, make sure that the flag was moved further than it was when you found it. If that is the only thing you do, than you did your part in this world.

Let me explain it again. Your masterpiece is key. Your masterpiece is needed in order to push this flag farther down the field for the next generation to push you even further and the generation after that, to push you even further, so we're impacting the world. We're leaving it better, so they have the chance to find their best self, to live their best life, and leave it better for the ones behind them.

Your masterpiece doesn't have to be able to be hung on a wall. It doesn't have to be able to be put in a museum. You don't need to put out red ropes in order to get a single file line set ready to see yours. Think of architects. Think of construction companies that build these massive buildings that we walk around and take pictures of. They take our breath away when we see them or see the view in which those buildings hold. Masterpieces are all around us every day and were created by those we call ordinary men for hundreds of years, but sometimes we forget they are there because we are so used to them. It doesn't mean what they did is less amazing. It means they moved the flag further for the next to make it even better. They did their part in hard hats and do not get the credit they deserve. That doesn't change the fact that they did their part for the greater good and created their masterpiece.

Most people don't look at construction workers and go, "Man, they're really making a masterpiece." But they are. They're making things we appreciate every day. We literally walk around Boston, New

York City, and L.A. and take pictures of buildings that are created by man that some look over and just see a construction worker. Construction workers paint masterpieces every day: the homes in which families sleep in and make memories in, the buildings people make livings in and careers in, the buildings in which people impact lives in, or the buildings that impact our lives. Everything matters and its all part of a masterpiece bigger than self.

Every line of work and every avenue of life is an opportunity to create your masterpiece. I think of coaches in many different sports from Coach Wooden, Phil Jackson, Vince Lombardi, and Bill Belichick, and the list can go on. I think of all of the people that not only made champions, but made men. The made great husbands and made great fathers. They made leaders in the community and successful businessmen. That's their masterpiece. It's not just being able to score a touchdown or hit the game winning shot. It's about being better as a person and to impact that many more people. Some will see a simple game. Some will miss the masterpiece, but some won't. If they reach one, they did their part, and believe me, from someone that has been in the sports world for some time, they sure have impacted more than one person.

You can't make anyone see anything; they have to be open and willing, but you can leave it there for the ones that want to, the ones that are willing to, or the ones that can see it, to be impacted by it. You can leave it there for the ones to feel empowered by it and to feel fueled by it, so that they can leave theirs. And so they can move it further for the next like you did for them. It might be hard to see, but that is what this is all about and what life is all about.

When I heard it said that we have this verse to contribute to life it made sense, "Life is a song, and we all are contributing a verse." What is your verse going to say? What message are you sending to the people that look up to you? What message are you sending to children, grandchildren, family members, friends, or the people in your local community? Whoever it might be. What are you telling them? How are you leaving them? Is that how you want it to be left?

We're all painting a picture here. No matter what life you live, no matter what line of life you live, and what area in life you live, we're all painting a picture. If we're all painting that picture, what is yours going to show them? Is it going to show someone that created their masterpiece? Is it going to show that was you were willing to unleash your greatness within to help the next and the next and the next, keep moving forward? Will it show your masterpiece was left to feel some sort of emotion, connection, or love, or was left to feel some sort of motivation or inspiration? Is it going to be to unlock their own creative ability or concepts in whatever line of life, or is your picture going to show someone that settled that didn't believe in themselves? Will it someone that wasn't willing to contribute to the song even though they had it in them? Man, I hope it's not that last sentence. What a shame that would be. You are here for more than that I promise you.

I'm sure you've heard me say it throughout this entire book. If anyone can, everyone can. I'm not even saying this is what we should do. I'm saying this is what we're here for. We're here to contribute to the greater good of it. You're painting a picture. You're putting a verse in a song. What are you willing to let that picture show? What are you willing to let your verse say? Is it going to be something that you want your kids, your family members, your loved ones, your community, or strangers to hear or see? Whoever it might be, is it going to be something you can be proud of, not only proud of what you did but what it allows others to do? Your masterpiece isn't just about you. It really has very little to do with you. It takes a lot of you, but it's created for others. That's what this is all about. What are we giving? What are we leaving?

Believe me, by creating your masterpiece, by going all out for it, by working your butt off for it, and by being willing to take the trials and tribulations that come your way, you will still accomplish your masterpiece and still push forward through the struggle. No longer will others get the reward but you will too. Also, others will be motivated by you and inspired by you to do their thing. People are looking for leadership everywhere. Will you be that leader for them to follow? For them to mimic?

I might try to make this sound easy, but I also know it's not. I know there are going to be days where we don't get closer to our masterpiece, days that we don't go 1 and 0. There are going to be days we lose. We can't let those days stop us, define us, or end us. Those days will come and sometimes come in rows. It will knock us down and at times try to keep us down. They will look past the failures. They will forget the titles. Most of the details will be left on the road side. What you leave will be what they remember. They don't remember you because of your position. Everybody knows who Abraham Lincoln is. Who's the 21st President? I know, go to Google. Find it, and then say it like you knew it. I ask that question almost everywhere I go. Very few times I get the right answer. Every time when they hear the answer they go, "Ah I knew it."

"No, you didn't. If you did, you would have said it."

Also, it's fine not to know it. He didn't leave the impact Lincoln did even though they had the same position.

We all know who Martin Luther King, Jr., is, but few people can name the people in the picture with him walking across the bridge. Why is that? They are all marching for their rights and future of this country. They are all in the struggle and trying to make it better. Actually, it is the same exact thing.

Everybody can tell you who Babe Ruth is for the most part, but very rarely, someone can tell you who batted before him even though he's a Hall of Famer and was on that same team as Ruth. Why is that? If it's what you do that's important, why is it? Why is it that we forget so many that do the exact same things that we can remember others for doing? It is because it's not what you do, it's how you do what you do. It's the impact you leave by doing what you do. We can bring up hundreds of examples in all lines of life where this is the case, but I hope you get the point by now.

How are you going to be remembered or how long are you going to be remembered? I say this phrase that was brought back because of a song, "Glorious" by Macklemore. He talks about how we experience death two times: once we physically die and then again when our names are said for final time by the last person who knew us. The ones that create these masterpieces, their names keep getting spoken. People aren't forgetting them. They aren't dying twice. They're living forever. Literally, if you look at it that way they are not dying. They are still living because their impact is still felt to this very day. Hundreds of years later, we are still in awe of their masterpiece.

My mom still tells stories of her great grandmother to my daughter, so my daughter has those stories that she's going to say about her great-great-great grandmother. She'll be living through her. Do not even get me started on the impact that my mother has made and how long she will remain in the hearts and actions of the people she has impacted. I am lucky I get to see real, live masterpieces being created right in front of me. My team, my mom, heck, even my daughter, Briana, to a point are inspiring me to go harder and further because how they are living and going for their best life. Look for it around you to keep you going for it yourself. We all need some inspiration or motivation here and there. Find it!

More importantly, are you creating that life, that impact, or that impression that generations are going to be talking about? Are you creating your masterpiece, so it won't be one of the forgotten masses that pass through this life without making the impact in which they were here to do. Most of our masterpieces fall on some day, and I just can't find that day on the calendar anywhere. Most of our masterpieces were "I will" until there were no more. They were great ideas. They were "could be" and they were "should be." They were will's and time until there was no time. I'm not saying this to be doom and gloom. I'm not saying this to scare you. Believe me, I don't think I have that power. I'm saying this to remind you that you have something great to contribute to all of us. The longer you hold yourself back from doing it, the higher chance there is we'll never get to experience it or to the extent we were supposed to. Neither one is acceptable anymore because now we know better. It's for all of us to do. It's for you to do!

I sit back and I wonder how many masterpieces can be made? How many great works of art, how many great songs, how many great literature works, how many cures to how many diseases, and how many smiles on how many faces could have been achieved and completed if the people that had it within them to do it, actually did it? How many more lives could be impacted? How many lives would be changed? How many people would get more time, deeper relationships, deeper meanings to their life and understanding of them, and a deeper appreciation to the things other than self? It's staggering how many things we might have missed out on because people weren't willing to go all in on themselves. They weren't willing to paint their masterpiece. They weren't willing to leave the impact. They weren't willing to be remembered because of a fear that they wouldn't be, but all that does is make it where it's a certainty you won't be. I pray I'm not one of those souls. I hope you're not either.

When I say your masterpiece can be anything, I want you to see who I'm talking about in this chapter. You might not know the first name, Milton, but I'm sure you've heard of the last name, Hershey. Yes, the founder of the Hershey Chocolate Company. He always talked about persistence and hard work because that's what carried him through life. No, it wasn't an easy street to chocolate, gold mines. Hershey left school early and did an apprenticeship, but only like in the movies, he lost a hat into a piece of machinery and was fired because of it in 1871, and at the ripe old age of 14. Then he went and worked in Lancaster at a candy factory until he decided his own business was the greatest idea he had. He opened a candy store near Philly just to see that business fail and fail bad. Surprised? The first store he opened wasn't Hershey. It was instant

Milton Hershey

success. It wasn't easy.

He moved around to New Orleans and Chicago but couldn't figure out the right opportunity. So in 1883, he settled in New York with a restaurant chain and a candy store named, Huylers. One point, a couple years later, he decided to quit, and he was going to sell chocolates and candies in the city of New York, which failed as well. He was so brokenhearted and demoralized from this, he moved back to the farm where he grew up in Lancaster, Pennsylvania. But, you know that little itch inside keeps pulling at you and tugging at you to do what you're supposed to do, to do what you are here to do, or you're meant to do. He started experimenting with chocolates and candies. He had a dairy farm and had some milk to play with.

In 1893, at 36, he established Lancaster Caramel Company which 7 years later, sold for $1 million at the age of 43, almost 30 years after dropping out of school and dropping a hat into a machine. Suddenly, that gave him the ability to start the Hershey Chocolate Company. When he opened their doors, he was still 43 years old. He is valued over 10 billion dollars now and is still remembered and enjoyed daily by many.

His success and his masterpiece did not come early in the adventure. It didn't come easily, and it didn't come without some scars. But everybody knows what Hershey Chocolates are. It's the most selling, best known brand, and the most famous brand of chocolates. His masterpiece was chocolates and candy and was the exact same thing he failed at and what broke his heart. It made him adjust his plan. To others, it looked like quitting, but it wasn't; it was adjusting to get back at it. His masterpiece was chocolate. Chocolate. His masterpiece is chocolates.

Think about that. Think of how much those chocolates mean to people, how they comfort people, how they excite people, and how they remind you of better times, different times, or good memories. They are the comfort you need during a painful point, or that boost you need when you're so close to accomplishing. Hershey just wasn't making chocolates and candies, he was making a way to impact lives.

He was making his masterpiece all the way down to the wrapper.

Some can say it's just chocolate or it's just candy. Others can see how amazing they are, what a work of art they are, what an impact they have, and how they'll be around forever or at least life times. Hershey will never die twice because his masterpiece was created. He was willing to bet on it. He was willing to go all in on it. He was willing to take the pain that went with going all in on it. He was willing to take the sacrifice, the struggle, the dedication, the rejection, the despair, the heartache, and the agony. He was willing to take everything that went along with it, and he was wiling to take it to accomplish it because you have to be willing. You do not have to be eager to go through it, but know it's part of the journey; it's all part of it.

So many people have painted amazing masterpieces. I'm not talking about with a paintbrush. I'm just talking about with their life. Mother Teresa, Oprah Winfrey, Bill Gates, Steve Jobs, Mark Zuckerberg, Abraham Lincoln, JFK, Martin Luther King, Michael Jordan, Lebron James, and the list goes on and on. None of them had the same thing in common: Beethoven or Mozart or Shakespeare or Edgar Allen Poe. They're all different, but it's all art. It's all a masterpiece. From the greatest cooks, to the greatest pilots, and to the greatest you, it's all about painting your masterpiece. It's about being willing and eager to get going at it and keep going at it. It's not just about settling, not just about quitting, and not just about putting your head down and not tucking your tail. It's not about being too scared to start. You have greatness within you. Just like all the people we talked about, if anyone can, everyone can. You can ... You just have to be willing to go through the journey just like Milton Hershey did.

Are you willing to go through it like Milton Hershey was? Are you willing to create the masterpiece like Hershey candies and chocolate is? Are you willing to paint the Sistine Chapel when everybody thinks it's an embarrassing failure, and it's not going to make it? Are you willing even if it takes too long? Are you willing even with all these other excuses and judgments they give you? Are you willing to build the most amazing buildings, have the most spotless floors, or create the greatest meal on Earth? Are you willing to make the greatest music ever heard or move someone to the point you change their life? Are you willing to write the most amazing poem or build the most fantastic home?

Whatever it is that you do, are you ready to create your masterpiece? Because we need you to. We all need that from you to make this place the best it can be, to make this life the best it can be, and to make me the best I can be. I cannot do it without you.

What's stopping you from creating a masterpiece? The only answer can be yourself. So, that is no longer a justifiable excuse. You will no longer accept you holding yourself back. You will now be your biggest cheerleader. You will now set the course to paint the masterpiece you are here to create that we all need you to create to move this place to where we need it to be, to be the best it can be for all of us, but more importantly, where it needs to be for you to live the best life you can as the best you possible.

Get your brush and start painting. If you already started painting it, keep going. No more excuses and no more holding back, it's time for us all to see your masterpiece. Honestly, I can not wait to check it out. I might not know you yet, but believe me, I will see your masterpiece. It will change my life for the better. So this is an early thank you from one of your biggest fans.

Chapter 14

The Dance

"Life can only be understood backwards; but it must be lived forwards."
- Kierkegaard

Looky, looky. Look how far we made it. This chapter I called "The Dance." Why? Because the dance is so encompassing. It's all a dance. We go back chapter by chapter and moment by moment in your life, and you put it all together; it's a complete dance. It might have started awkwardly, but you got better as it went on like most things honestly do.

Everyone knows the song "The Dance" by Garth Brooks in which he talks about not wanting to have regrets and that no matter how it worked out, this life was worth it. The song speaks to the fact that it might not all go perfect or even end how you desire. It might not go the way you want it to. It might not go as planned, but the dance is worth it. The chance is worth it.

This is all worth it. Another thing you have to know is you are worth it. You are worth all this. You're worth every single second of it. When I said I'm your biggest fan, I mean it. I'm one of your biggest fans. If you're reading this right now, you're in this moment, and I'm one of your biggest fans and will be for the long haul.

Feel free to reach out. Listen, you can connect to me in a million ways: my number, my email, and my information is made public on all my social media accounts for a reason. I want to be able to connect with you guys. So connect with me at Coach Mike Fabber on almost every platform of social media there is.

I am sure the cornerstone of all this, of our existence, is connection. We want to connect with people, places, and things. So if we have an opportunity to connect with one another, I'm all about it; let's do it.

So, do not hesitate to reach out. I will be there. I will respond, and it will be me. It will not be anybody that's part of the team. It will be me because that's how much you mean to me. That's how much all of this means to me. This is my calling, and I'll answer the call.

You have greatness within you, and we all need it out of you. If that means you living your best life as the best version of yourself for us to be able to get what we need to keep moving this thing forward, to get the next verse of the song, to be able to be inspired or motivated, to add to our fire, and to be our fuel, whatever it is, we need it. And we need it from you, each and every one of you. So, tell the people around you too. We need it from them. The more that you do this, the better we all are and the better chances we all have.

So, let's look back at our time together in this book. "F the Norm" because there is no normal way. You can put whatever word you want for "F," "forget," or any other one as the "F" of this book, but really what I named that for wasn't for the shock and awe.

It's for how tired I am of hearing "It's not in my cards. It's not for me. Ah, this isn't my life. This isn't how it was supposed to go. That's not what I'm supposed to do even though I desperately want to."

I'm tired of all those excuses and all those reasons because they're wrong. There's not something special in our DNA that makes us be able to do greatness. It just takes the burning desire to grow and to go all out for it. That's it.

Now, does that mean everybody knows your greatness now? No, everybody doesn't know the Sistine Chapel, and that thing's amazing. Everybody doesn't know your favorite song, but it's moved you. It's impacted you. That person's masterpiece in that song has changed your life, and that's huge.

When they create one's meal and give it away, I think a chef forgets about if that person was hungry or not. The memories they can create over it, where it could take them back to, or the emotions it can make them feel through a simple meal, that's their masterpiece. And it's impacted lives.

So, whatever it is you do, go for it. Whatever it is that's gnawing at you, whatever it is that makes your heart leap when you do it or just even think about it, go for it. When you know it's your thing, a smile gets permanently pasted on your face when you're about to attempt it, or know you're going to, or when you're doing it. That's what you're meant to do here. That's what you're here for. It is your calling or purpose as they say.

In the chapter "Calling," we went over this. I mean, you have that thing. Go all out for it. Don't hold anything back for it. There are no excuses for that one. Go do your thing. I can't say it enough. I can't plead with you enough. I can't beg you enough. I can get on my knees and implore you until the end of time for you just to go do your thing because that's what we need of you. That's what you're here for. So, go do it, and do it often.

You know, I sometimes run into people with families, and they say, "Well, listen, I have a family. I can't do that."

And I always respond with, "What message are you sending to your family? Not to go after your dreams? Not to take the call for your purpose? Not to fulfill your destiny? What message are you sending?" Do not use them as your excuse to settle. They deserve better from you. Heck, you deserve better from you.

I'm not saying you should quit your job, and I'm not saying put everything on the market. I'm not saying just leave everything. In no way, shape, or form am I suggesting that. Not all masterpieces are created by single, childless men or women. These things were created by people with families. You can still do it.

I'm not saying rush naively into the dark with a spoon for battle. You have a powerful brain. You're a powerful being. Use it. Develop your tools and skills along the path to your destination.

Spend 8 to 10 hours on someone else's dream and spend zero on yours. I don't think that's the message you want to send, and I don't think that's the sucker you are. Those days are done now. You read this, Gin. Those days are over.

You're going to find time and space to do your thing and keep building it till that's your thing that makes you what it makes you. If it's a side-hustle, if it's just done out of love and extra time and just given away for people to experience, whatever it is, that's what it's meant for.

But you're meant to do it at the level where it impacts lives. The greatest things about you are meant to be shared with others. That's what you're here for. Do what you're here for. Be willing to do it. It takes courage. It does, I know. I get you. Don't worry. I understand. It takes a whole lot of courage, and you're going to be very vulnerable.

Check out Brené Brown in leadership and courage, and she'll tell you everything you need to know about vulnerability and leadership; she's got it on lock down. There are a million other people that have such powerful messages that we all need to hear a time or two.

So, don't be afraid to listen. Don't be afraid to go for it. What's the worst that can happen? You're still here. You're still doing your thing. You're still all about it, and that's what it is. That's what it's for.

So, I'm going to review backwards because why would I do anything the way you expect. There is no norm, remember? "F the Norm." So, I'm going to go backwards. Paint your masterpiece. You know what I mean! You got it. This world is your canvas. Make it.

I remember when I was a basketball coach. Reporters would stop by here and there and ask me questions about players and coaching. I would tell them about coaching and what it took. I would portray it as an artist, and I'd say, "The court is our canvas, and the players are our tools. They are our paintbrushes and different shapes, forms, sizes, and all different colors. But they all come together, and they paint our portrait."

This life is your canvas. All your resources are your tools, your paintbrushes, the paints, et cetera. Make that masterpiece. Paint your portrait, and whatever it is, paint it. All of it. Every single piece you have to do. Make it even if it means you won't see it at the end and even if it means you won't see the appreciation that comes from it or the masses it moves.

It's not what it's about. And when you're on, I'm sure it feels great, but it's not what it's about. It's about adding your verse. It's about doing your part. It's about being the best you and living your best life, and there's no way you can create a masterpiece without doing that.

It starts with you; that's the great part because you're you, and you control that, which I'm sure we already talked about in other chapters. Here I'm being like a country music freak because I keep bringing up country songs. But Chapter 12: "Timmy" is about being humble and kind.

It's not about telling the world what you do. It's not about other people even recognizing it when you want them to recognize it or appreciating it when you want them to appreciate it. As great as that would be for you, it isn't for that. It is for something so much greater than that.

It's not about them doing the things you believe they should or feels right to you. It's not about if they screwed you over or not, if they paid the due that you paid or not, or if they gave what you gave or not.

Listen, I know a lot of people around me that have not. I know people that forget when you do things for them, forget who had their back, or will change and make up stories in their mind. We all know those people that will make up false narratives just to make them right and you wrong.

Do not fall into that game. That game's a loser's game. There's no winning at the end of that, and it just takes up a massive amount of time and space in your mind and even worse, your heart. Don't let it.

Stay humble, and stay kind. Give to people. Give people chances. Help people, especially if no one helped you. Help people because that's what they should have done for you, and that's what you were hoping they would do for you. Help people because its in your soul. Not just good for it.

Even if no one did, you still do it for the next person because you're better than that. You're bigger than that. Your purpose is bigger than that. Who you are is bigger than that. As hard as it is to remember, do not lessen your value, your worth, or your character for someone else's lack of it.

Believe me, this was one of the hardest things for me to learn: I always wanted to get to the people that got me. I always wanted to screw the guys that screwed me. I always wanted to prove the point that they didn't win, and I won. It sounds horrible typing it and reading it, but it is true.

All I was doing was taking time and energy and so many different emotions and feelings and putting them into something that meant nothing, so much so that the other person probably didn't even think about it. And they might not have won, but I definitely didn't win because I gave that time that I could never get back. I gave that emotion that I could never take out of my heart. The impact will always be there.

I think of the scars it created, the marks it left behind, and so many things it took from me that I'll never get back because I let it. Not only did I let it but also I was the cause and leader of it. So, it's not about them. It's not about the due. It's about you and what you do.

So, don't let them change you. Don't let their actions make you something. In the words of the American poet and rapper, Sean Carter, aka Jay-Z, "What you eat don't make me shit." The only person that makes you anything is you.

So, no matter what they're doing, live your life the way you're supposed to live it and the way you're meant to live it. Whatever their issues are is just theirs, and how they want to live their life is theirs. How you live your life is yours. Just stay humble, and stay kind, like Timmy said.

Chapter 11: "Serenity," is named after the Serenity Prayer. Accept the things you cannot change. You know, like those things in your life, your past, and your history that you cannot change — the things that have happened to you have happened, whether they were good, bad, or indifferent. Where you are right now is where you are right now.

The only thing that will change that is what you do next. Heck, the only thing to change that is what you do right now. You can't go back. You have to accept what has happened. You can't hang on to it. You have to accept it because the longer you hang on, the longer you try to fight the past, and the longer you're stuck in it.

That means you're not painting your masterpiece. That means you're not going forward or growing forward. That means you're not living your best life as the best version of yourself. Heck, that means you're not even getting closer to it.

And what a shame to live stuck where you don't even want to be, so accept where you've been, what you've went through, and who did what. Be willing to move forward, to move on, and to live. The greatest payback is to live the greatest life possible for you even if you are stuck on something you did because you do not want to be that person. Perfect, don't be! Change it now, and keep going. We have all made mistakes and have done things out of character. What defines you is either the mistake or how you come back from it. You pick.

Think of it like this. I'm sure there are people that have done great things for you. I'm sure there are people that have rooted for you. You might not want to pay attention or acknowledge it. That's fine, but it's happened.

There are people that have helped you along the way. Believe me, I have numerous people that have helped me along the way. I'm forever thankful for that moment they did.

And I also have people that have screwed me along the way. I have. I can't change any of it. I'm thankful for all of them because they've all impacted my life. And fortunately, I have to keep moving forward because if not, there's no chance I get to where I want to go.

Change things you can. You can change the trajectory of your life. You can change the path of your life. I was reading something today about that the person with the past doesn't dictate the person of the future.

They were talking about the character that played Iron Man, Robert Downing Jr., and how he was incarcerated for drug abuse and maybe some other misdemeanors and little things but mostly, drug abuse. And now, he's like one of the most respected actors and one of the highest-paid actors for his character in Iron Man.

Your past doesn't dictate your future. It doesn't hold you back. It doesn't keep you down. It only does if you let it. So, be willing and have the courage to change the things you can. Be willing to go for it. Be dedicated to creating you and the life you desire.

And the hardest one for me is the wisdom to know the difference. I spent numerous hours, days, months, and years trying to change things that I knew I never could.

I've spent time accepting things that I could change. I wasted time, plenty of it, and time is something we'll never get back. The most precious resource is time. We'll never be able to get it back. That bank account will forever go down, and I was wasting it because I didn't have the wisdom to know the difference.

I didn't have the understanding. I didn't gain the education, and I'm not talking about what grade I graduated from. I wasn't able to know what battles I could fight and change and what battles I had to just accept as is to keep moving forward, to not let it stop me in my path, and to not let it delay my life.

So, accept the things you cannot change. Have the courage to change the things you can and the wisdom to know the difference. It's the Serenity Prayer. Look it up. It's real. I pray it for you and me every day.

The next chapter is "Vision." Have your vision. I don't mean just your eyesight. Have your vision. What's your next month going to be like? What's your next 6 months going to be like? Plan it out. What's your next year going to be like? What's your next 3 years going to be like? What's your next 5 years going to look like?

And listen. I know it's going to change. It's not going to be i-dotted or t-crossed perfect. I get it, but have a vision for your life. Have a vision for every aspect of it, and I mean every aspect.

These are things I talk about with my clients. I tell them: "What's your best relationship? What does your best relationship look like? What does your best friendship look like? What does your best relationship with your family look like? What does your best relationship with your romantic partner look like or your child look like?

What does your best relationship with a co-worker or your community look like? What does your best relationship with every piece and character in your life look like? What's your greatest vision of your career or your profession? What's your mountaintops? What's your vision for it all?

Because, listen, if you're in a relationship that's not that, can you make it the best relationship? Can you change some things to make it what you want, or is it the time to move on because it's not?

See? It's all about your vision, and if you don't see it, how can anyone else see it? And if you don't see it, how do you know where you want to go towards? How do you know what's next? How do you know if you don't see it? How do you know what direction you want to go in and where you came from? What are you evolving into?

In Alice in Wonderland, Alice tells the the Cheshire Cat, "I don't know where to go." And the cat said, "Where do you want to go?" Alice says, "I don't know." He's like, "Well, then, go either way. It doesn't matter."

Because if you don't know, it doesn't matter, but if you don't know, you don't have the directions to go. You don't know the choices to make that will push you in that direction.

So, you need to have your vision, and it has to be clear, knowing that it'll adjust and knowing it'll change in time. It's okay, but you have to have some sort of map to go off of to start, and you can always adjust it. But there has to be a map to know which way to go.

There is always a starting spot. There's always a finish line. There's always a first step and a last step to connect because you need them to be able to get the in-between done. So, have your vision and see your endings.

Now, they can always be adjusted. They can always change. I've said that, and I'll say it again: don't think this is final. This isn't the end when you make it there because believe me, I've had mountaintops that I've accomplished, and when I was climbing it, I saw another mountain I wanted to climb. So, I climbed it and then started doing the other mountains I noticed on the way up.

They say the midget on the shoulder of a giant can see farther than the giant. Listen. While you're becoming who you want by going through the accomplishments that you're going through to become it, you're going to start seeing further. More things are going to be possible in your mind and to you in general.

Your mind's going to be open to more; you're going to be able to do more, and you're going to have more confidence because you're accomplishing things along the way. So, have that vision and start accomplishing.

Your vision's going to grow. It's going to expand. It's going to change. That's a good thing. That's a great thing because it means you're growing. It means you're climbing. It means you're getting closer. It means you're getting higher. You're getting closer to that best you living that best life. So, have your vision and make that thing 20/20 or better.

The next chapter, which I already mentioned numerous times in most of these other chapters, is about growing. Better yourself everyday in everyday possible.

Listen, you're like a plant. You have to give yourself some water, and you have to give yourself some sun light. Now, you have to have nutrients in the soil because you have to grow and feed yourself.

You can't be this person you are today, tomorrow. You can't be the person you are today, next month. If you are, you're doing an injustice to yourself and everyone around you.

I'm not saying you have to go to college. I'm not saying you have to go to get an education in school. I'm not saying that. You can read, and if you don't like reading, you can listen to audiobooks. If you don't like audiobooks, you can watch short videos on YouTube now. There is a million and one ways to do it. So, do it!

There are a million conferences to go to, including the Unleash Unow conference. So, the best way to grow is to come out and check us out. Shameless plug: got to love it.

But there are conferences, and there are clinics and summits. There are all kinds of events and tools that are used that could just make you see more, make you know more, and to make you learn and become better. Because you can't be the best if you don't become better because this is not the best version of yourself.

No matter how much you might think it is or try to claim it is, this isn't the best version of yourself, and it's not the best version of your life. If you think it is, you're fooling yourself , and that's it.

There's no one around you that believes it, and I don't care who you are, Bill Gates down to my brother.

Whoever you are, you are not leading your best life. I'm not saying it's a bad life, but it's not your best. You still have more to do. You still have the best you, so you're going to grow to become it. The best is ahead if you make it possible.

I love John Maxwell, but I disagree with him in this one. He said, "You don't accomplish goals anymore. You just grow. No goal setting. Just grow. If you grow, you'll get everything you want." That part I agree with, if you grow, you get everything you want and keep growing.

The part I don't agree with is not having goals because you don't accomplish goals if you set them. You grow to goals. You don't accomplish goals; you grow to goals.

When you set a goal, you're not capable of doing it yet. Why? Because you aren't there yet. You're not the person to do it yet, but then you start bettering yourself and growing til it's possible.

Let's say if your goal is to make varsity baseball, but you can't hit the fastball. So, you go outside, and you hit baseballs for an hour every day. Then all of a sudden, you make that varsity team.

It wasn't because you were ready when you sought it. It wasn't because you were ready when you made it a goal. It's because you grew every day to the goal. You grew to the goal. You grew till you could do it.

So, grow. Grow as often and as fast as you can. Grow. Gain it all. Take it all in. Take as much sun in as you can. I don't mean that in a literal sense because I don't want you to get any kind of a skin disease. But as the plant, take it all in. Soak it all up and grow to your max.

Every day, look for opportunities to grow. Go to a conference, a clinic or weekend getaway, whatever it is. Read the book. Listen to the audiobook. Watch the video. Whatever the heck it is, grow by learning your best way. Do it and do it as often as you can. Another John Maxwell line: "You don't have to do it all day, but do it every day." So, grow.

I love this next chapter. It is called "Your Job." When I read it back, I was like, "Man, Did I even talk about people's work?" No, I didn't. I read a little bit, and I was like, "Oh, man, I like this. This is on point." And very few times I like anything I do. Believe me. I'm my hardest critic.

But you are your job. Your job is you. It's not anyone else's job. It's not anyone else's job to support your goals. It's yours. Now, willing people can appreciate your goals because not everybody will. But it's no one's job but yours.

It's no one's job but yours to make your life as great as it can be. It's no one's job but yours to make your relationships work. It's no one's job but yours to get you down the career path you want to get to.

It's no one's job but yours to make your family work, to make your relationship with your parents work, or to make your relationship with your friends work. It's your job.

So many times and so often I hear people say, "Well, they did this, or they wouldn't do this." "This happened with this," or "This made this job this tough." "This job was so hard because of the resources, and people didn't care." Ah, it's not their job. It's your job. Stop looking for others to do your job!

And it stops when you stop having these expectations and these built-in excuses for what's happening in your life. You just start taking ownership of it, of all of it. You just start taking accountability for it all.

Jocko Willink is an amazing person. Check him out and thank him for his service if you ever get the opportunity. He has a book called Extreme Ownership. I love the book. I think he named it wrong. I think it should be called The Right Ownership because in the that, he talks about all truth.

Own every part of your life. Own it all. Why? Because it's yours. Don't give anyone else the power in your life, and don't give anyone else the reason to be the excuse for it. Don't do that. You are you. You are your job. You are completely up to you. Your life is completely up to you. You are the master of you.

Yes. Bad things are going to happen. Yes, you're probably not going to get every job you go for. Yes, you might get fired from your job. Yes, you might get dumped, left, or divorced. Yes, your family might not talk to you, and you won't have the relationship that you seek. Yes, you might not have the friendships you want. Yes to all of that.

All of it is your fault. Well, maybe not. Will Smith says, "Not your fault, but it's damn sure your responsibility," so, we'll go with that. This all might not be your fault. It might be everybody else's, but it's still your responsibility.

It's still your job to make this hand, the hand you're dealt and the greatest hand ever played because it's the only one you get. So, adjust, change, check, grow, and do all the great things, but do them because it's your job and no one else's. Don't expect anything.

Here's the next chapter. It's the toughest chapter for me ever in anything I ever written or talked about in any presentation I ever gave. It made me smile a little bit just because of the fact that I could write it. It means I'm healing more, so I found the good in it. I saw my growth.

But this one was tough. It is called "The L's of Life: The Suck." Embrace the suck. Listen, we're all going to have the suck. If you try to do great things or try to do nothing, you're going to have the suck. If you try to live this amazing life or if you try to live the most ordinary of lives possible, you are going to have the suck.

The suck is guaranteed. The suck is promised. The suck is coming, and if you experience some of the suck, you're probably going to experience more of it. I'm sorry to be the bearer of bad news, but it's true. The suck is real, and the suck is coming for you.

And when everything is riding high, the suck's probably coming. And when everything is riding low, there could be more suck around the corner. Let's totally prepare for the suck. Right? Let's face the suck and totally accept that the suck is here, the suck is real, and the suck is coming.

The suck is part of the Ls of life. We have lessons which we all too often learn, and we normally learn by going through something shitty most of the time. We normally learn by going through some crap. I like to call it the river of shit, and I have very small paddles. But that's sometimes the only way we get it. It makes us see the lesson in it.

In the book, I use the example of when my family restaurant burned down. Foolishly, when I'm running something, I think I know best, and I was very stubborn in my opinion (also youth). I didn't have the insurance we should have had, so we lost a couple hundred thousands of dollars. Boy, that sucked. Let me tell you.

It sucked even more so cleaning up the building and counting the dollars lost. Everything and anything was gone. Barely anything was salvageable. All the merchandise and the equipment, from the TVs to the bottles of booze, to the stuffed freezers to the fridges full of food, to the walk-ins to the stove, and to the dishwasher equipment was destroyed.

So, it wasn't in the cards that we could even get near the money we lost, and I had to own that one. I had to own that one to my family. I had a young daughter at the time. I told my mom she could retire and do her own thing at the time.

I took a loss, the lesson type, the L of life. I took a financial hit, and it impacted everybody. And I have to own that, and I have to take that. That was a lesson I learned. Now I know not to be foolish. Even though I don't want to, I pay the insurance just in case, so everybody doesn't pay for my shortcomings.

The other L in life is loss. I'm not talking about financial loss; this is way worse. That's why I said "financial hit." After you've experienced a couple losses, you start calling everything else lessons.

I'll never forget that feeling, knowing that one of my best friends wasn't going to ever talk to me again, and I wasn't going ever see him again. And I am actually doing this, writing this on the anniversary of his death. That's tough. That's hard.

I remember that moment I knew something was really wrong, and my life wasn't going to be the same forever. I woke up on the couch and saw my mom on the floor crying. I saw my dad sitting and saw my sister standing crying.

And like I said in my first book, I had the option to close my eyes and to stay in my dream as long as possible. I could have pretended like I didn't know or walked towards my nightmare of my greatest fears. That's when I found out my brother was no longer with us.

I had to face my greatest fears again when my dad passed when I was a teenager, and Matt Alan passed as a teenager. And again when my boys, Wiggins and Ferris, passed away the last couple years. Those are losses. Those are the type of losses you don't get over but learn to live with. They are part of my motivation and inspiration every single day to get better and impact more lives.

I think when I was doing nothing, when I wasn't living my best life or even trying to, and when I wasn't the best version of myself or even trying to become it, I experienced some of those losses, most of them. Then when I decided that I wanted to be better and tried to become the best me, or to become the best me I could be, living the best life I could, I experienced some as well.

So, there's no protecting you from these losses. I wish I could, believe me. I wish could protect myself and all of you from it because I know how painful they are. But if I'm going to get them either way, and if you're going to get them either way, and if everyone's going to have them either way, you might as well try to hit back with the same impact or greater that life is going to hit you with.

You might as well try to make such an amazing story and leave such a forceful impact, so that it makes all the losses worth it, makes all the pain worth it, and the trials and tribulations worth it. Because if not, what was the point?

If not, what are we here for? Just the L's? The lessons and losses? No, I want to be here for more of the W's, the wins, some of the M's, the miracles, and some of the A's, the amazing. I want all the fantastic stuff too, and I know we could go get that.

The other ones are going to come to us. But the great, we are going to go get because if we have to experience the L's either way, believe me, we are going to experience both.

Just being here, we signed up for the L's. We have to go accomplish the W's. So, be willing to go. Embrace the suck and go earn those W's. Make all of this worth it.

The next chapter's perfect for following this: "Pazenza." My grandmother used to say that all the time, "Pazenza. Pazenza, Michael. Pazenza." My mother used to tell me all the time, "Pazenza, Michael. Pazenza." And if you don't know Italian, that means patience, and clearly, I needed generations of it.

Mountains take time to be conquered. Becoming the best you takes time. Living your best life takes time. Creating your masterpiece takes time. Growing takes time. All these things take time and plenty of it.

I see people that want to do amazing things and 6 months later, they wonder why they haven't. Because it was only 6 months. I know people that want to be presidents of companies that worked for them for a year and wonder why they're not. I know people that have lofty goals, and they're supposed to but have no concept of the time it takes to get them.

I know people that have these big mountains to climb, and that's great. But like Simon Sinek said, "You've still got to climb the mountain. You can't just see the peak. You've got to be willing to climb." And the climb takes time. John Maxwell said, "Everything worthwhile is uphill."

And so, pazenza. Have some patience. Be willing to go through, to grow through, to get through, and to get to where you want to be. I'm all about you being the best you living your best life. That's why I say it so many times. But I also need you to know that's going to take time, but it's going to be worth it.

Answer the phone! No, it's the next chapter. It's "The Calling," the one your meant for. There's a reason why some things just make your heart leap like we talked about. There's a reason why you get all excited for certain things. There's a reason why you have these hobbies and why you find time to do these different activities or crafts.

It's because it's trying to tell you you're here for it, and that it's your calling. Be willing to answer the phone. You're not here to do anything that doesn't help you create that masterpiece.

No, I don't care if you're a street sweeper if that's your calling. If you get excited that you know kids are going to go out and play on a safe street and not have broken glass, tobacco, or other things that could be harmful or just negative for their life, then it is your calling.

If you know they're going to have that and you could be the one that makes it where they don't, that's your masterpiece. That's freaking awesome, and thank you for it.

Well, if that gets you excited and if that's what gets you out of bed, it is your calling. One of my favorite quotes, by me, is that, "Your alarm clock wakes you up, and your why gets you out of bed." Your passion and your calling will get you out of bed. It will be stronger than any coffee.

It'll move you forward. It'll show you where you're supposed to be. It'll push you towards it. It'll do all those things; it's meant to, and it's worth it. Believe me, but you've got to answer the call. You've got to be willing.

It might not come right away, and it can change in time. Believe me, I think we were here to answer more than one call and to do more than one thing. That's part of our masterpiece, and that's why I don't say do the one thing to create your masterpiece. That's why I never label one part of your life that's your masterpiece.

It's all part of it. But you've got to be willing to answer the call because it's calling. Believe me, the phone's ringing. You've just got to go on and answer it.

And choices. Oh, you have the choice to answer the call or not. Choices are huge: squad goals, the people around you, and the choices you make to have who's around you. The choices you have in your life determine who's around you during your time here.

Believe me, I've screwed this up. First, we've all made wrong choices. Don't to try to act like we haven't. I've made some of the worst choices.

I've trusted some of the worst people. I've backed some of the worst people. I've backed people that didn't give a dang about me backing them that forgot I've done it.

I think now they think they deserve and earned everything that was given to them by their people, including myself, as part of what should've been done for them, rather than being appreciative of what is. And they're the people you shouldn't have around.

There are choices you have to make, and some are hard. Listen, to grow and be the person I wanted to be, I had to say bye to some people that were near and dear to me.

Not, "So long," not "I can't talk to you," but "I can't hang with you like I used to. I can't interact like we used to. I've got your back. I'm here for you if you need anything, but I've got to keep going in my direction. And you not approving of that or accepting that makes it where I've got to disconnect to a degree, at least."

And I know I said this is all about connection, but it's about the right connections. It's not about the wrong connections. So, those wrong connections creep in and cause us pain and agony and change the trajectory of our life and our choices.

But one of the most important things, one of the biggest choices you make are the people you're going to have around you. Your squad, your team, your circle, or your family is key. Whatever you want to call it, the people you have around you the most are critical for your life.

Someone once said, "Show me five people. If four are millionaires, I'll tell you who'll be the fifth." They said, "Show me five people. If four are losers, I'll show you who'll be the fifth." That's how important the people you hang out with are.

You'll never go further or higher than the people in your circle. You will go up together. So, if they can't fly that high or if they're not willing to, now here's your choice, are you not going to?

Because listen, I have people that disconnected from me for whatever reason they did, and I'm not sitting here saying, "Man, how could they do that?" I'm sitting here saying, "Man, I hope they get everywhere they want and everything they want." They'll get as high and as far as they wanted to just like I hope the ones that I did it to say in return, "I hope he got everything he was going for."

But pick the right circle and pick the right crew. Have the right people around you with the right mindset, with the right attitude, and with the right go-getter engine inside them and what fuels their fire.

Because some guys I know, it's all partying at the club, and listen, I loved the club for awhile. But it didn't fuel my fire anymore, so I couldn't go. I didn't want to go. It wasn't bettering me. It wasn't getting me closer to where I wanted to be. It wasn't living my best life as the best version of myself, so I had to X it out of my life.

Then the people I was with that would go there all the time, well, they got mad. They said, "Are you too good for us now?"

"No. This is not the lifestyle I want to live. This is not the lifestyle I want to lead. It's not who I am anymore. I've grown." So, make your choices right and pick the people around you carefully.

This is the chapter I brought up the guys that almost got me locked up for over a decade. That is how important picking the people around you is. Your life and freedom can depend on it.

The next one, one of my favorites, reminds me of old-school Disney. "Mirror, Mirror." We talked about the finish line. We talked about where you're going. We talked about how to connect the dots, and there are two points you need: your vision of the end, where you are right now, and who you are right now.

What kind of person are you? What kind of father or mother are you? What kind of brother or sister or son or daughter are you? What kind of co-worker are you? What kind of community member are you, or whatever else position you have in life? And just what kind of person are you, in general?

And where are you, right this moment? Where are you in the life that you want to have? Where are you on the path that you want to go down, or are you even on that path? Where are you at this very moment? Listen, this isn't a knock on you. This isn't a feel-bad for you. This isn't to discourage you before you start kind of moment.

This is a be brutally honest. This is a starting line. And listen, the more brutally honest you are, the better because it's going to be more impressive and the further you're going to go because of it.

Because you have your mountaintop, you have your vision, and you have your starting line. And that starting line's normally not very high or not near where you want to be.

That's the journey. That's the climb. And that's the making the right choices. That's the answering the call, and that's where the patience part comes in. And that's going through the suck, and It's you being your job and growing to the goal, like we talked about. I know all these chapters make sense when you put them all together. I mean that's the point. When I looked at over 100 highly successful people from all walks of life, you see these chapters in most of their stories.

But know where you are and what you're doing right now. Know it all, but be honest. Be completely honest about where you are. And that's "Mirror, Mirror," because you've got to look in the mirror; you cannot lie about what you see.

You've got to tell yourself: "Listen, I'm not the person I want to be; I drink too much. I'm not the person I want to be; I'm not home enough. I'm not the person I want to be; I'm just working this nine-to-five job without passion or care, and it's affecting every aspect of my life."

If those are the truth, say your truth. And say exactly where you are, make your starting line, and be brutally honest, as painful as it can be, because you can take it.

You know why? Because like Chapter 2 says, "You have thick skin." One of the greatest skills I believe to have now is the ability to have thick skin and to be able to take criticism, to be able to take "hate," and to be able to take all the criticism because there's going to be critics everywhere now. They love throwing shade at everyone and everywhere they can.

Social media has made everybody a critic. Everybody can say it like their expertise is in every aspect of life. They're going to give it to you, and listen, they're going to be brutal about it.

People can be brutal. Not everybody's going to like you. Not everybody's going to believe in what you are doing. Not everybody's going to believe in you.

Like Brene Brown wrote about and President Theodore Roosevelt said, "It's not the critic who counts; not the man who points out how the strong man stumble, or where the doer of deeds could have done them better. The credit belongs to the man who is actually in the arena, whose face is marred by dust and sweat and blood; who strives valiantly; who errs, who comes short again and again; who spends himself in a worthy cause; who at the best knows in the end the triumph of high achievement, and who at worst, if he fails, at least fails while daring greatly, so that his place shall never be with those cold and timid souls who neither know victory nor defeat."

Meaning: pay no attention to those in the cheap seats of life like author Brene Brown mentions in her book, Dare to Lead.

Get the thick skin. Handle that shit and keep moving forward. You can take it. You were made for it. This isn't time for sensitivity. Those times are over. This isn't time for poor me. That time is over. That is a pastime that no longer exists in you.

Now it's time for kick-ass you. Now it's time for you to take names and take numbers of those challenges you conquer and the ones that try to get in the way. Heck, now it's time to not let anyone get in your way. Because you have the scars built up and the thick skin; you've received this over time, and you've went through worse than they could ever put you through.

I would say I wish the most painful thing was what people thought about me. And listen, most of the time what you think, people aren't thinking that much of you. They won't talk about you that much. You're not thought of that often, and it's okay. Hell, that's even better.

But have the skin to handle it. Build the toughness to handle it.

Keep pushing through. Develop that toughness. You're going to need it, especially on your journey and if you want to accomplish great things. People are going to try to stop you from doing it. I don't know why. I don't understand it either, but we don't have to understand it. That isn't the job we signed up for, but we already know that.

We just have to live our best life as the best version of ourselves. We just have to grow to the person we are meant to be and who we are supposed to be. That's our job.

You is your job. Your job is not everybody else, not what everybody else thinks of you, or why they even think it. None of that matters to you. You are your job. Have the thick skin to be able to do you.

In Chapter 1, day one, we're here now. You've started. Day one. And maybe when we first started this and when we talked about it, maybe it wasn't.

But now you have it all, now that you see it all. You hear all the stories of what they've done, and you know how all the people accomplished great feats. You can do it too because if anyone can, everyone can.

So, today is day one, wherever you are in your journey and whatever day it is. But even today, even if you've already taken steps, today's day one of this you, of this mindset, and of this growth.

This is day one, and I'm excited for you because you're on the way to create your masterpiece. You're closer to it. You're closer to the you, you want to be and the best version of yourself. You're closer to the life you want and the best life you can have.

You know more. You're prepared better than ever for it. You're mentally ready to go through the battle for it, and you know it's worth it. Today is day one. You've got your starting line. You have your finish line. Start connecting your dots. Start living the best life, the life you are here to live.

It's the best you. Grow to that thing. Become that thing. Be that thing because it's what you are here for. It's your calling. It's your purpose. It is you!

I'm so freaking proud of you that you got to this point. I'm excited for you to see what it holds, and I cannot wait to see your masterpiece. Thank you so much for taking this journey with me. It means more than you know.

Do not be afraid or shy to reach out. Do not be afraid or shy to email me or call me. Do not be afraid or shy to send me a picture of you holding the book.

Believe me, I love this stuff. Connecting with people on deeper levels than just bogus BS means the world to me. That's what I'm here for. So, do not be shy to do it. Do not be afraid to do it. I long for it. Seriously, from the bottom of my heart, thank you. Thank you. I can't say it enough. Thank you.

Now you're ready. Actually you saw that you were always ready for this. You're prepared for it. It was in you the whole time, but now you know it. You're capable of greatness. Not only are you capable of it, you have it within you already, waiting to be tapped and unleashed on this world for all to see. No holding back anymore. Go all out now. Go for it.

It's worth it, and more importantly, you are worth it. Thank you again. Until next time, peace, love, and happiness from Unleash Unow family. Peace.

www.ingramcontent.com/pod-product-compliance
Lightning Source LLC
LaVergne TN
LVHW051518070426
835507LV00023B/3180